STRIPPED DOWN:

Piece by F*cking Piece

Lindsay-Michele

ISBN (Paperback): 979-8-9993155-0-2
ISBN (eBook): 979-8-9993155-2-6
ISBN (Hardcover): 979-8-9993155-1-9

www.lindsay-michele.com

Dedication

For the ones who saved me—
with love, with presence, with no need for words.

For the ones I lost—
but still feel every single day.

For the ones who made me a mother—
the reason I kept going when I didn't think I could.

For the version of me that survived—
when it would've been easier to give up.

And for the woman I am becoming—
*I am so f*cking proud of you.**

Trigger Warning / Author's Note

This book is not just a story.

It's a truth that was never supposed to be told.

It talks about emotional, psychological, physical, and sexual abuse.

It touches on trauma, PTSD, and the kind of pain that doesn't always have language.

If you're still deep in your own healing, please go gently.

You don't have to read this all at once.

You don't have to agree with every word for it to be valid.

You don't have to be ready to face everything right now.

You just have to know you're not alone.

What's in these pages is **real**.

It's *unfiltered*.

It's what **abuse feels like**.

And what healing really looks like—

not the version people post online.

If it's too much, pause.

Take a breath.

Come back when you're ready.

Acknowledgements

To my mom-

Losing you changed everything. Nothing has felt the same since — and maybe it never will. But somehow, I still feel you here. In the quiet moments. In the strength I didn't know I had. In the pieces of me you helped shape — even the ones that broke.

You were my safe place. The one person who saw me completely — without ever needing an explanation.

I miss you more than words can ever explain. Some days the ache feels impossible. But even through the hurt, I still talk to you — because I know you're here. **I feel you with me, every single day.**

I love you. I always will. And I hope you're proud of the woman I've become — even with all the cracks and scars — still standing, still trying to turn all this pain into something that matters.

To my dad and my brother Brian-

Thank you for being the ones I never had to heal from. You have no idea how rare that is. In a world full of people who took and twisted and left me doubting myself, **you were steady. You were safe. You were real.** Thank you for showing me that not all men destroy softness, that some actually protect it.

I love you both more than you probably realize.

To my kids-

You are the reason I'm still here. Not just the reason behind this book. You are the reason behind everything. You've been my anchor in the storm, my steadiness in the chaos, and the only thing that's ever made me feel truly grounded. You didn't just give my life meaning. You gave my healing purpose. You are my greatest love. My biggest accomplishment. My why. **The love I have for you almost aches in my chest — it's that deep, that real, that powerful. And everything I've built, everything I've become, is because of you.**

I share my story to heal — but also to help make sure you never experience what I did, by saying the things no one warned me about, by breaking the silence that keeps people stuck, and by showing you that **you never have to question your worth. That your voice matters. And that your voice is your greatest power.**

To the ones who chose truth over silence-

You saw the truth. You trusted what was right over what you were told. You didn't have to look closer. You didn't have to care. But you did. **You showed up — when no one else would. You stood by what was right.** And your support... the reminders that I wasn't crazy... it's meant more than I can ever explain.

Thank you for seeing me.

To Doug Henry-

I don't believe we cross paths by accident. The universe has a way of placing the right energy in our lives at the exact right time. You've been a reminder of what real peace feels like. **Thank you for always holding space for me, and bringing calm to the chaos when my soul needed stillness.**

To every person who shared their story with me, messaged me after a post, or opened up about their own pain-

Your courage reminded me why this work matters so deeply.
You helped me feel less alone in my own journey.
And in every word of this book, I hope you *feel* **seen**, **validated**, and truly **understood.**

This book is for all of us!
Who are still finding our way back to ourselves, *piece by f*cking piece.*

To the version of me who kept surviving in silence-

You did it all alone for so long. Bracing for impact. Waiting for the next betrayal. Trying to earn love. Trying to prove your worth. But in the middle of the darkest season — you stopped reaching outward and started reaching inward. You found something deeper. **You found stillness. You found you. And somewhere in that quiet... you realized you were never really alone.**

The universe had you the whole time. You are love. You are light. You are enough. And you always have been.

To the ones who abused me, and to the people who thought they could break me-

I have to live with the scars you left. The PTSD. The triggers. The reminders of just how cruel people can be. But you didn't break me. **I found a way to turn my darkness into light** — but not for you. The only light shining in your direction is the one that exposes exactly who the f*ck people like you really are.

You reap what you sow.

Why I Wrote This Book

I didn't write this because I reached some healed or enlightened place.
I didn't write this because I figured it all out.

I wrote this because I needed somewhere to put the pain.

Because for years, I carried it alone.
And when I say alone, I mean *alone* in the truest, most terrifying way.

I had been emotionally, mentally, verbally, sexually, and physically abused
in different relationships by people I trusted.

Some of it looked like screaming and chaos.
Some of it looked like silence, control, and manipulation behind closed
doors.
Some of it looked like affection, followed by destruction.
And some of it looked like me dissociating while someone did what they
wanted with my body — like I didn't even exist.

It wasn't just one person.
It wasn't just one relationship.
It wasn't just one moment.

It was years of betrayal.

Years of gaslighting.

Years of explaining myself and still being misunderstood.

Years of thinking, *maybe it's me.*

Years of spiraling.

Years of giving everything and still not being enough.

Years of trying to survive the damage they left me with, while still being blamed for the mess.

I wasn't pretending to be okay.

I wasn't functioning in silence.

I was breaking down constantly.

And no one was listening.

Two years ago, I hit a place I never imagined I'd reach.

I was empty.

So emotionally and mentally destroyed that I honestly didn't know if I could keep doing life.

I wasn't depressed.

I was *done.*

Done carrying it.

Done trying to explain it.

Done being the one holding all the weight for what other people did to me.

I had been trying for so long, doing everything I could just to stay above water.

And eventually, I just couldn't anymore.

As I lay on my floor in tears, just sitting in all the pain I had been carrying because I couldn't hide it anymore — it was in that moment, the darkest time of my life, that I chose me.

That's when the healing started.
Not because I was ready.
Not because I had a plan.
But because I didn't have another choice.

I started meditating.
I started looking into trauma.
I started asking questions like, *what actually happened to me?*

Because at that point, I genuinely didn't even understand it.
I couldn't name it.
I just knew I wasn't okay — and hadn't been in a long time.

I wrote this book because when I was trying to piece myself back together, I had no blueprint.

I didn't have anyone handing me a book like this saying, *Here. You're not crazy. You're just healing from abuse no one ever taught you to recognize.*

And I desperately needed that.

I needed someone to explain what emotional abuse really feels like.
How physical abuse doesn't always leave bruises where people can see them.
How manipulation makes you believe it's all your fault.
How sexual violation inside a relationship still counts.
How trauma doesn't just go away because you left.

How you can love someone who destroys you.

How you can still miss them.

How healing is a f*cking spiral.

How recovery doesn't look like peace and yoga and gratitude.

It looks like rage.

It looks like shutting down.

It looks like dissociation, confusion, body memories, shame, fear, and exhaustion.

It looks like fighting every day to show up for your kids or your job or yourself — and still questioning if you're ever going to feel normal again.

I didn't write this to sound brave.

I wrote this because I had to.

Because I was sick of carrying it in silence.

Because I knew if I didn't get it out of me, it was going to keep eating me alive.

This isn't some pretty collection of inspirational thoughts.

This is what abuse *actually* does to you.

What healing *actually* looks like.

What survival *actually* costs.

It's not for the ones who got a clean ending.

It's for the ones still unraveling the mess.

Still triggered by the tiniest thing.

Still rebuilding.

Still grieving the version of themselves they lost.

I wrote this book because *I* needed it.

And I hope if you're holding it —

you feel less alone.

Less crazy.

Less ashamed.

More seen.

More understood.

More ready to come home to yourself — piece by f*cking piece.*

While this book is written from my perspective as a woman —

it's not just for women.

It's for anyone who's ever been —

silenced, manipulated, or made to feel like they were never enough.

For anyone who's —

questioned their worth, lost themselves in a toxic relationship, or tried to rebuild from rock bottom.

If the truth in these pages speaks to you —

then it was always meant for you.

This is your story too.

Contents

Chapter One

You're Not Broken — They Were Just Manipulative as Hell

You Think It's You

At first, you think you're the problem.

You overreact.

You're too emotional.

Too needy. Too much. Too dramatic.

You try to shrink yourself.

You question your memory.

You apologize for things you didn't even do

—just to make the tension stop.

Because somehow, it always comes back to you.

"If I just communicate better, maybe he won't get so cold."
"If I stop overthinking, maybe this will work."
"If I can just be what he needs... maybe I'll finally be enough."
But you never were the problem.

You were just being conditioned to believe that you were.

It starts slowly.

You find yourself rewriting texts three times before hitting send.

You rehearse conversations in the mirror, convincing yourself not to "sound crazy."

You reread your own words wondering how they'll twist them this time.

"I don't even know who I am anymore."
"I feel like I have to earn basic decency."

"I never know which version of them I'm going to get today.".

This is how it begins.

Not with violence, but with silence.
Not with shouting, but with shame.
Not with a slap, but with a look that makes you crumble inside.

You start to monitor your tone, your face, your breath
—because being too much could mean another day of being punished
with silence, coldness, or guilt-tripping.

That's not love.
That's survival mode in disguise.

If you've ever found yourself spiraling after a normal conversation, wondering if you accidentally triggered a storm
—you were never the unstable one.

Manipulation Doesn't Always Look Like Abuse

There were no fists.
No bruises.
No dramatic public outbursts.

So you told yourself it wasn't abuse.

But that's the f*cked up part—manipulation wears a mask.

It looks like love at first.
It feels like care.
It hides behind concern, behind "just being honest," behind jokes that make you feel small but somehow make them look charming.

It looks like:
• The silence after you opened up about something vulnerable.
• The sarcastic comments that left you laughing on the outside and gutted on the inside.
• The fights you didn't start but always had to end by apologizing.
• The way they "forgot" your boundaries—but remembered every little thing you did wrong.

"I'd sit in the car after work, just breathing—prepping myself to walk into the house."

"It wasn't a war zone, but it was never peace either. It was walking on eggshells with a smile."

And the worst part?
They made you think you were the toxic one for noticing any of it.

If you brought it up—you were "too sensitive."
If you cried—you were "trying to manipulate them."
If you pulled back—they claimed you were "punishing" them.

That's not a disagreement.
That's not miscommunication.
That's psychological warfare wrapped in gaslight-scented gift wrap.

You didn't imagine it.
You didn't make it worse.
You were reacting to real harm—with a nervous system that was doing its f*cking best to keep you alive.

"If you're still questioning whether it was abuse—ask yourself this: why are you the only one who came out of it doubting yourself?"

Because They Trained You To

This wasn't random.
It wasn't bad luck.

You were trained.

Bit by bit, they shaped your reactions.
Not with love, but with punishment.
Not with support, but with withdrawal.
Not with care, but with control.

You didn't stay because you were weak.
You stayed because you were conditioned to survive in chaos.

Every time you hesitated before speaking up...
Every time your chest tightened when their mood shifted...
Every time you changed your opinion to avoid a fight...

That wasn't "overthinking." That was training.

"I stopped asking for anything because I was tired of being made to feel guilty for having needs."
"I started praising the bare minimum, because anything more felt like too much to even hope for."
"I remember the exact moment I realized I was scared of their silence more

than their anger."

They didn't have to say, *"You're not allowed to feel that."*
They just rolled their eyes.
Dismissed you.
Withdrew affection.

That's how it works.

You were taught that expressing hurt makes you the villain.
That crying is "too much."
That standing your ground means you're "trying to start a fight."

They rewired you—to flinch instead of speak.
To appease instead of stand up.
To doubt your own damn feelings.

And the sickest part?
You probably still feel guilty for leaving.

But you weren't dramatic. You weren't unstable. You weren't impossible to love.
You were reacting exactly how someone reacts when their nervous system is stuck in survival mode.

Let's Call It What It Was

They weren't "just stressed."
They weren't "emotionally unavailable."
They weren't "bad at relationships."

They were manipulative as f*ck.
And no, you're not being dramatic for saying it.

They gaslit you.
They made you question your emotions, your memory, your truth.
They turned every disagreement into a crime scene where you were always
the suspect.
You were left cleaning up their emotional messes, patching up the damage,
and blaming yourself for bleeding.

"He made me believe I was the one who needed help."
"I kept thinking if I was calmer, sweeter, quieter—it wouldn't get this bad."

And let's be real—sometimes you were screaming.
Sometimes you were angry, messy, reactive.

Because when someone spends months (or years) pushing you into a
psychological corner, of course you're going to come out swinging or
collapsing.

That's not who you are.

That's who they trained you to become under pressure.

So let's stop calling it "a toxic dynamic" and name it for what it was:

• Emotional abuse
• Psychological manipulation
• Control masked as concern
• Love used as leverage

It doesn't need bruises to be real.

It doesn't need screaming to be harmful.

It doesn't need a police report to leave you shattered.

Just because they never hit you doesn't mean they didn't destroy you.

Confessions You've Never Said Out Loud

These are the thoughts that haunt you at night—the ones you've never dared say aloud because part of you still wonders if you're the crazy one.

"I was terrified to make them upset—but didn't even realize how scared I was until it was over."
"I used to rehearse conversations in my head before bringing up anything."
"I had to ask if it was okay to cry."
"I still flinch when I hear the same notification tone on someone else's phone."
"I started Googling: 'Am I emotionally abusive?' because I believed everything was my fault."

These are the kinds of truths that get buried under years of self-blame.
But every one of them is valid.
Every one of them is real.

It wasn't all in your head.
You didn't make it worse.
You weren't just "too emotional."

You were emotionally starved, gaslit, dismissed, and left drowning in guilt for simply needing clarity, love, and safety.
That's not an overreaction.
That's a trauma response.

And the longer you hold these truths inside, the louder the shame gets.

So let's speak them.

Let's scream them if we need to.

Let's stop whispering truths that should've been acknowledged from the start.

Because saying them out loud?

Is how you take your power back.

When Love Becomes a Weapon

At first, they were magnetic.
Charming. Thoughtful.

They said the right things. Held you close. Looked at you like you were magic.
They mirrored your hopes. Matched your energy. Made you feel seen.

And then... they weaponized it.

Suddenly that same love came with conditions.
• Conditional affection
• Conditional safety
• Conditional support

You were loved—but only when you weren't too much.
You were safe—but only when you didn't challenge them.
You were heard—but only if what you said didn't make them uncomfortable.

"He used to tell me I was 'his person'—but made me feel like I didn't matter at all."
"She said she loved how emotional I was—until she used my vulnerability against me in every fight."
"He told me no one would ever love me like he did—and he said it like a

*f*cking threat."*

They baited you with a version of love you'd never had before—then slowly chipped away at your ability to feel worthy of it.

You weren't asking for too much.
They were offering crumbs and calling it a feast.

Real love doesn't feel like a high-stakes negotiation.
Real love doesn't punish you for your pain.
Real love doesn't demand you stay silent to be safe.

If You're Still Making Excuses For Them...

Let's pause here. Seriously—stop.

Because you've been carrying the weight of their story on your shoulders long enough.

"He had a rough childhood."
"He doesn't know any better."
"He's not like this with other people."
"It's because he loves me so much."
"He didn't mean it."
"She's just scared of being vulnerable."
"They're trying, they really are..."

No.

Intent does not erase impact.

You don't have to hate them.
You don't have to seek revenge.

But you do have to stop handing them permission slips to keep hurting you.
The longer you protect their image, the longer you delay your healing.

"I kept defending him to my friends—while secretly praying they'd tell me to leave."

"I said 'he's just complicated' so many times I started to believe abuse was just part of love."

"I stayed quiet about the worst parts because I didn't want anyone else to think less of him. Meanwhile, I was slowly disappearing."

You don't owe anyone silence when it's your pain that paid the price.

You are allowed to tell the truth—even if it makes them look bad.

You are allowed to stop protecting the person who never protected you.

The Damage They Won't Take Responsibility For

You didn't just "get your heart broken."

You got rewired.

Your nervous system got hijacked.

Your sense of self-worth got demolished.

Your ability to trust—even yourself—got shattered.

You flinch at kindness now.

You brace for abandonment in silence.

You sabotage good things because your brain thinks safety is dangerous.

And they?

They moved on like nothing happened.

Posted smiling selfies.

Played the victim.

Told their side of the story first—because they always knew how to manipulate the spotlight.

"He told everyone I was the problem—while I was too broken to even speak."
"I didn't just lose a relationship—I lost pieces of myself I'm still trying to find."
"I walk around in a body that feels foreign. Like it's still stuck in that house. That voice. That silence."

They won't say sorry.

They won't make it right.

They probably won't even admit it happened.

But that doesn't make the damage any less real.

The aftermath is yours to carry—but the guilt isn't.

The healing is yours to do—but the responsibility for the harm is theirs.

Read This Again, and Again, and Again

You weren't broken.
You were betrayed.
You were manipulated.
You were gaslit, ghosted, guilted, and gutted.

But you are **not** the damage they caused.

You're what survived it.

"I kept thinking I was the mess... but it turns out I was the mirror."
"Every time they told me I was hard to love—I loved harder."
"I thought I lost everything. But I was actually shedding the pieces of me that were never mine to carry."

You don't have to prove how bad it was.
You don't need anyone else to believe you.
You don't need to defend your healing.

The fact that you're still standing?
Is the most powerful f*cking truth there is.

So say it again—louder this time:

It wasn't me.
It was never me.
And I'm done carrying the shame they created.

Pause.

Take a moment to be still.
Just breathe.

I AM WHOLE AND WORTHY.

MY PAIN DOES NOT DEFINE ME — MY STRENGTH DOES.

Chapter Two

Red Flags You Weren't Taught to Notice

The Ones That Didn't Look Like Red Flags

You think you'd notice abuse, right?
You think it'd be loud.
Obvious.
Scary.

But it wasn't.

It looked like sarcasm.
Like jokes at your expense.
Like long silences when you were upset.
Like *"Why are you always so sensitive?"*
Like rolled eyes when you tried to talk about your feelings.

It looked like your needs being too much.
Your dreams being unrealistic.
Your boundaries being a *"problem."*
You weren't taught that those were red flags.
You were taught they were normal relationship issues.

You were taught to compromise.
To be chill.
To give the benefit of the doubt.

So you did.
And that's how it started.

You Excused It — Because Everyone Else Did Too

The truth is, most of us were never taught what actual manipulation looks like.

We thought abuse meant bruises.
We didn't know it could mean emotional withdrawal as punishment.

Or constant sarcasm that only ever cuts one way.
Or someone who only shows affection when you're compliant.

You don't notice the red flags when the world has colored them beige.

"He didn't yell. He didn't cheat. He just made me feel small… and I stayed because no one told me that was enough of a reason to leave."

And when you tried to explain it to people, they looked confused.

Because it didn't sound bad enough.
Because you were still functioning.
Because you had good moments too.

So you kept doubting yourself — while the damage just kept building.

The Body Knows First

Before you ever found the words for it — your body already knew.

It knew when your chest tightened every time he picked up his phone and went silent.
It knew when you walked on eggshells without even thinking about it.
It knew when you couldn't breathe unless the mood in the room was *"good."*

You thought it was anxiety.
Or maybe your trauma.
Or maybe you just weren't healed enough.

But it wasn't you.

Your nervous system was reacting to danger before your mind was ready to accept it.

That was your intuition.
Your gut.
Your power.

And they taught you to ignore it.

You'd wake up already anxious and didn't even know why.
You couldn't explain the pit in your stomach.

You just knew something was off — and kept telling yourself you were overreacting.
You ever notice how you started narrating things in your head before you said them out loud
— just to make sure they wouldn't sound *"crazy"*?

You learned to self-edit before you even spoke.
You'd reread your texts ten times.

Pause before asking questions.
Convince yourself not to care so much — just to avoid being called *"too emotional"* again.

And the silence?

It wasn't peaceful.
It was punishment.

You knew the difference.

You could feel it in the way your body braced for it.
You could feel it in your stomach, in your chest, in the way your jaw stayed tight for days.

"He's Just Going Through a Lot"

Let's talk about this one.

Let's talk about all the excuses we were taught to make for red flag behavior:

- *"He's just under stress."*
- *"He's never been taught how to express emotions."*
- *"His ex really messed him up."*
- *"He doesn't mean to hurt me."*
- *"He's working on it."*

They're always working on it.
Always *"about to change."*
Always giving you just enough to doubt yourself and stay.

But real change?
Doesn't come with manipulation, control, or blame-shifting.

If they treat you like shit but keep telling you they love you — believe the treatment, not the words.

The Red Flags They Don't Put on Checklists

Let's name a few no one talks about:

- They say *"you're overthinking"* every time you bring up your feelings
- They call you *crazy*, then ask for nudes two hours later
- You feel drained after being around them
- They remember things you did wrong but *"don't recall"* anything they did
- You're exhausted just trying to be *"enough"* for them
- You spend more time confused than calm
- You keep explaining yourself — over and over — and they still don't hear you

You start managing their moods instead of living your life.
You stop asking questions just to avoid the cold shoulder.
You track their tone more than your own emotions.

If it leaves you constantly questioning yourself — **it's a red flag.**

Your Heart Isn't Broken — It's Waking Up

You don't have to defend the moments you missed it.

You were conditioned to miss it.

Your survival brain wanted to believe the good moments were real.

Because they were.

But they were also weaponized.

Love shouldn't feel like whiplash.

And if it did?

You weren't broken.

You were surviving in a relationship that only worked when you stayed small.

"You're not naive for missing the signs. You're human for believing the version of them they showed you first."

Confessions From the Fog

- *"I didn't think it was abuse because he never hit me."*
- *"I thought my trust issues were the problem — not his lying."*
- *"I kept telling myself, 'It's not like he's screaming at me,' even though his silence was louder than a slap."*
- *"I blamed myself for everything — even while I was slowly dying inside."*
- *"I didn't even realize how afraid I was of him until I felt peace again."*
- *"I would cry and apologize — for crying."*

If any of that feels familiar — you're not alone.

You're not weak.
You're not stupid.

You were just lied to by someone you trusted — and trained to second-guess your own alarm bells.

If You're Still Unsure...

Here's how to know if it was a red flag:

• If you had to explain your pain and they still didn't care
• If you adjusted your personality just to avoid arguments
• If you lost your spark, your joy, your voice
• If you're still unraveling what the hell even happened

Then yes — it was toxic.

Yes — it was abuse.
Yes — your feelings are valid.

Even if you loved them.
Even if they had good traits.
Even if you still miss them sometimes.

You can love someone and still acknowledge they were emotionally unsafe.

Let's F*cking Name Them All

Emotional Manipulation

- They only show affection when you're easy to handle
- They withhold love when you set a boundary
- They cry when you're mad — but never when they hurt you
- They use your empathy as a weapon
- They make you feel like you broke them
- They guilt you into staying by saying *"no one else would put up with them"*
- They spin your past against you and call it *"transparency"*

Gaslighting & Mindf*cking

- *"I never said that."*
- *"You're remembering it wrong."*
- *"You're so dramatic."*
- They act like you're crazy for reacting to their behavior
- They rewrite the story to make themselves the victim
- They make you doubt the abuse while you're still bleeding from it
- They twist your words until you don't even trust your own voice

Control Dressed Up as Love

- They call it *"protection"* but it's really control
- They get mad when you talk to friends or post something *"too revealing"*
- They make decisions for you, then call it *"leadership"*
- They isolate you *"because no one else gets you like I do"*
- They demand access to your phone, your location, your life
- They act like you owe them your body, your time, your peace

Covert Abuse

- They compliment you in ways that feel more like insults
- They get quiet — not to reflect, but to punish
- They do *"nice"* things just to guilt-trip you later
- They make jokes about your trauma and laugh when you flinch
- They never apologize — only deflect
- They keep you stuck in a loop of *"maybe tomorrow he'll be better"*

Guilt Trips & Shame Games

- *"After everything I've done for you..."*
- *"I guess I'm just the worst then, huh?"*
- *"You never appreciate me."*
- They cry the hardest when you're finally strong enough to walk away
- They say *"you've changed"* when you finally find your f*cking boundaries
- They act like your healing is an attack on them

Trauma Bond Traps

- You crave their validation even though they're the one who broke you
- You defend them to your friends who saw the truth
- You remember the *"good times"* and ignore the chaos
- You feel addicted to the cycle — even when it's killing you
- They beg you to stay, then punish you for being *"too much"*

Passive-Aggressive Bullsh*t

- They post cryptic stories clearly about you
- They *"forget"* things that were important to you

- They joke about cheating and say you're insecure when it upsets you
- They weaponize silence and make you apologize to break it
- They use sarcasm like a knife
- They act annoyed every time you need something

Bonus Red Flags That Still Count
- You feel worse about yourself the longer you're with them
- You second-guess every text you send
- You cry more than you laugh
- You're scared to bring things up because of how they'll react
- You try to *"be less sensitive"* instead of asking them to stop being cruel
- You've thought *"Maybe if I just..."* more times than you can count

Read This Again

Sometimes you didn't even fight back — not because you agreed, but because it felt safer to let them believe they were right.

And you hated yourself for that.

For going quiet.
For saying *"it's fine"* when it wasn't.
For staying.

But let's be real:
You weren't staying because you didn't see the red flags.
You were staying because you didn't feel safe enough to leave.
And that's not weakness.

That's survival.

They trained you to confuse love with tension.
To confuse chemistry with anxiety.
To think the sick feeling in your gut was your fault — instead of a warning sign your body was begging you to hear.

"I started calling it overthinking — but it was really my intuition screaming."
"I couldn't tell the difference between loving them and fearing them."
"I thought being uncomfortable was just part of being in love."

Even now — after everything — you still second-guess yourself.

You wonder if you're being dramatic.
If maybe it wasn't that bad.
If it was somehow your fault after all.

But read this again:
If they made you shrink, question your reality, abandon your needs, and apologize for your own boundaries — it wasn't love.

It was manipulation.

If they only loved you when you were convenient — that wasn't connection.

That was control.

If your nervous system is still recovering — the damage was real.
If you still miss them but feel relief they're gone — that's not confusion.
That's clarity finally cutting through the fog.
So stop waiting for someone else to validate what you went through.

You know.
Your body knows.
And that truth is enough.

Say it out loud — again:

It was abuse.

And I don't need anyone else to believe it before I start healing.

Pause.

Take a moment to be still.

Just breathe.

I TRUST MY INTUITION.

I HONOR THE SIGNS MY SOUL HAS BEEN QUIETLY SCREAMING.

Chapter Three

Not Just the Ex —
Manipulative as F*ck Runs in
Families Too

The Abuse That No One Wants to Admit

When we think about abuse, we think about the partner.

The *narcissist*.

The gaslighting ex who broke us down.

But what if the damage didn't start there?

What if you were already living in survival mode before you ever loved the wrong person?

What if your nervous system had already been rewired to mistake *chaos* for love?

What if, long before you ever ended up with someone who manipulated you, you were already primed to question your *worth* by the very people who were supposed to build it?

Here's the hard truth no one talks about enough:

Sometimes, the most manipulative people in your life share your last name.

Not every abusive relationship starts in adulthood.

Sometimes, the most brutal emotional damage is done in *childhood*—by the people who were supposed to protect you.

The parent who guilted you for having needs.

The sibling who constantly competed with you.

The "loving" relative who used your kindness to control you.

The household that made you question if love and pain were the same thing.

We were trained to see it as normal.
As *family*.
As culture.
As "how we were raised".

But let's stop sugarcoating this sh*t.
It was **emotional abuse**.

When Family Is the Original Mindf*ck

They fed you, clothed you, maybe even told you they loved you.

But they also ignored your tears.
Mocked your emotions.
Controlled your choices.
Invalidated your voice.

Made you apologize just to be heard.

One minute they were praising you.
The next, you were the enemy for speaking your truth.

You weren't loved—you were *managed*.
And your silence was the currency that kept the peace.

If love felt like fear, anxiety, or walking on eggshells,
You weren't being raised.
You were being **programmed**.

Programmed to stay small.
Programmed to people-please.
Programmed to second-guess your every feeling and need.

You learned early that approval was conditional.
That love had *rules*.

That your emotions were too much unless they were convenient.

And when your caregivers were also your gaslighters,
you didn't just question the moment
—you questioned your *memory*.

You started doubting your instincts.
Dismissing your emotions.
Silencing your own gut.

You grew up surrounded by people who claimed to love you—but only the version of you that didn't make them uncomfortable.

You weren't nurtured.
You were emotionally monitored.

And every time you tried to grow beyond the version of yourself they could control, you were punished—subtly or overtly—until you learned to shrink again.

"But They Were There for You…"

Sure.

Maybe they put food on the table.
Maybe they paid for your college.
Maybe they stayed married "for the kids".
Maybe they made sacrifices.

But that doesn't erase emotional abuse.

Because love isn't just about what's given.
It's about what's **withheld**.

You know what wasn't there?
Safety.
Affection.
Unconditional support.
Accountability.
Respect for your feelings.

You're allowed to acknowledge both things:
• That they did some things for you.
• And that they also f*cked you up in the process.

Both can be true.

But only one of them still haunts you at night.

Only one of them still shows up in your triggers, your relationships, your anxiety, your inner critic.

You're not ungrateful for naming the hurt.
You're just not pretending anymore.

The Family Dynamic That Trained You to Stay Small

In some families, speaking up is a crime.
Expressing emotion gets you mocked.
Asking for respect earns you silence.

And calling out dysfunction? That gets you *exiled*.

So you learned early how to:
• Shrink your presence.
• Numb your feelings.
• Keep secrets.
• Apologize for things that weren't your fault.
• Smile when you wanted to scream.

You were taught to *survive* love, not receive it.
So it's no wonder you tolerated toxic relationships.

Your brain had already linked "love" with walking on f*cking glass.
You normalized pain.
You tolerated emotional starvation.
You mistook emotional breadcrumbs for *safety*.

Because when pain is familiar, it feels like home.

Even if it's **hell**.

The Parent Who Was Always the Victim

This one's subtle.

Maybe it was the parent who cried whenever you tried to bring up something they did wrong.
The one who turned everything around and made you feel guilty for speaking up.
The one who used phrases like:
- "After everything I've done for you..."
- "You're so ungrateful."
- "You're the reason I'm like this."
- "I didn't have a childhood either."

You learned to **self-abandon** just to make them feel okay.
You stopped having needs because it hurt too much to express them.
You shrank every time you needed comfort—because needing anything made you the *problem*.

They didn't want to raise a child.
They wanted an emotional support human who never challenged their behavior.

This is emotional neglect dressed up as *martyrdom*.
It's guilt masquerading as love.
And it leaves wounds that are invisible to outsiders—
but bleeding in silence inside of you for years.

You didn't get to be the child.

You were their caretaker, their confessional, their emotional sponge.

And no one asked if *you* were okay.

And now you're here, trying to unlearn all of it.

Undoing the belief that love means sacrificing yourself.

Untangling your worth from their pain.

Realizing you weren't "too much"—they just never made space for your full humanity.

The Sibling Who Was the Golden Child

Let's talk about sibling abuse.

Not every sibling is a safe space.
Sometimes they're your first bully.
Sometimes they're the weapon your parents use to invalidate you.

The one who could do no wrong.
The one who got praise for your ideas.
The one who laughed when you cried.
The one who mirrored your trauma but blamed you for reacting to it.

You weren't crazy for noticing the difference.
You weren't "jealous".
You were **othered** in your own damn house.

They could get away with everything.
You got punished for breathing wrong.

And if you still flinch at their tone, still feel like the black sheep, still get
dismissed at family gatherings—
you're not being dramatic.

You're remembering.
You're remembering the *microaggressions*.
The invisible battles.

The loneliness of being surrounded by people who never really saw you.

That's how deep the programming runs.

You blamed yourself for the lack of connection.

You wondered what was wrong with you.

Why you weren't enough.

Why love seemed effortless for them but *conditional* for you.

But here's the truth no one told you:

They weren't better.

They were **chosen**.

And you were sacrificed.

You were the emotional scapegoat in a system that needed someone to carry the shame.

The Invisible Scars You Carried Into Adulthood

You grew up learning that being good meant being quiet.
That love meant sacrifice.
That boundaries were betrayal.
That speaking your truth was an attack.

So when you entered adult relationships, you didn't recognize the red flags—because they looked like *home*.

You ignored the gut feelings.
You gave more than you had.
You over-explained.
You apologized for taking up space.
You mistook control for care.
You confused pain with passion.

And people wondered why you stayed.
But they didn't see the blueprint you were handed.
The one written in guilt, gaslighting, and generational trauma.

Why Cutting Ties Hurts Like F*ck—But Heals Like Fire

Nobody talks about how grief hits when you cut off family.
Not because you miss the abuse.
But because you finally see what you never had.

You grieve the support that never showed up.
The protection you didn't get.
The love you thought was real.

And sometimes the hardest part is knowing they'll never own what they did.
They'll never say sorry.
They'll never change.
They'll go on like nothing happened.
Or worse—they'll play the victim for losing you.

But guess what?
You didn't leave to hurt them.
You left to save yourself.

That's not selfish. That's *sacred*.

And the grief doesn't just hit once.
It comes in waves.
On birthdays.

On holidays.

When your friends talk about their parents or siblings.

When your child asks why certain family isn't around.

When you realize you know how to comfort others but have no idea how to receive it yourself.

You're not just grieving people.

You're grieving the *future* that could've been.

The parent or sibling you wished you had.

The family you needed.

The version of family you always hoped would show up.

And yet—

the moment you chose truth over loyalty,

your healing began.

You Don't Owe Anyone Your Loyalty If It Costs You Your Sanity

Let's burn this into your nervous system:
• You are not required to stay connected to people who hurt you.
• You are not disrespectful for speaking your truth.
• You are not responsible for protecting people's feelings over your own healing.

If the only way to keep the peace is to betray yourself—that's not peace. That's *performance*.

Let them be uncomfortable.
Let them gossip.
Let them rewrite the story however they need to sleep at night.

You know what happened.
You know what it cost you.
And that's all the permission you'll ever need to walk away.

Healing doesn't require their approval.
It only requires your *truth*.
Even if your voice shakes.
Even if your hands tremble.
Even if your family calls you crazy.

You don't need their permission to reclaim your sanity.

The Guilt Will Come—Expect It, Don't Obey It

You'll hear their voices in your head:
- "You're breaking this family apart."
- "You're so cold."
- "You used to be so sweet."

And part of you might even believe it—because guilt was your leash for years.
But healing means remembering this:
Guilt doesn't equal truth.
Just because you feel bad doesn't mean you're wrong.

You're breaking generational cycles.
Of silence.
Of emotional manipulation.
Of calling trauma "tradition".

You're the one who finally f*cking said it out loud.

And yeah, that makes you the villain in their story.
But that also makes you the **hero** in yours.

And hero work is never easy.
But it's worth every ounce of freedom it buys you.

You Don't Have to Keep Playing the Role They Assigned You

Maybe they called you the "sensitive one".
The "difficult one".
The "too much".
The "dramatic".
The "selfish".

But that's not who you are.
That's who you became to survive in a home that didn't make room for your full humanity.

You don't owe them your silence.
You don't owe them your energy.
You don't owe them anything.

You get to walk away.
You get to stop performing.
You get to build your own damn peace.
And you get to be loved in a way that doesn't require you to *disappear*.

Final Words (That Younger You Needed to Hear)

You weren't a bad kid.
You weren't too emotional.
You weren't a burden.
You weren't crazy.

You were *hurt*.

And instead of being held, you were gaslit.
Instead of being seen, you were controlled.
Instead of being nurtured, you were manipulated.

But you're here now.
Sifting through the rubble.
Naming the wounds.
Loving yourself the way they never did.

And if no one ever told you this:
You didn't deserve any of that sh*t.
And you never have to go back.

You get to heal loudly.
You get to feel deeply.
You get to f*cking exist—fully, freely, and finally.

Pause.

Take a moment to be still.

Just breathe.

I AM BREAKING CYCLES.

I AM REWRITING

MY FAMILY'S STORY WITH COURAGE AND CLARITY.

Chapter Four

When Fake Friends Feel Like Family — Until They Don't

The Ones Who Claimed They'd Never Leave

Not every wound comes from someone you dated.
Some come from the person you trusted with your *deepest* pain.
The one who said, **"You're like family."**
The one who stuck around for your darkest seasons — and then used your trauma as a punchline when you started to heal.

Let's talk about those people.
The ones who weren't lovers, but left you just as **f*cked up**.
The ones who got close, only to turn cold the moment you stopped playing small.
The ones who made you question your worth in the name of *"just being honest."*

Because betrayal doesn't always come with romance.
Sometimes it comes with a best friend necklace.

It's the ones who cried with you.
Who swore they'd never be like the others.
Who showed up just long enough to get your trust — and then twisted it when it was no longer convenient.

You didn't see it coming, because you *believed* in them.
You held space for them. Defended them. Loved them like family.

But family doesn't weaponize your vulnerability.
And love doesn't vanish when you start to grow.

What Fake Friendship Actually Feels Like.

Here's how it creeps in:
• You start feeling anxious when their name pops up on your phone
• You second-guess your good news before sharing it
• You downplay your pain to avoid being called dramatic
• You realize you're constantly the one checking in, listening, fixing, supporting — but never being held yourself
• You feel lonelier with them than without them — but you keep trying anyway

It's subtle at first.
You tell yourself they're just busy. Or blunt. Or going through something.
You keep giving them the benefit of the doubt — because that's what *loyal* people do, right?

But deep down, you know:
This isn't what friendship is supposed to feel like.
You're emotionally starving in a relationship that calls itself **"loyal."**
You're shrinking yourself to keep the peace.
You're calling it *"connection,"* but it feels more like performance.

Because real friendship is supposed to feel like **home**.
Not like a test you keep failing.
And you shouldn't have to keep sacrificing your own needs just to feel close to someone who only shows up when it benefits them.

The Jealous Friend Who Claps Quietly

Some people don't clap when you rise.

They get quiet.

Weird.

Distant.

Passive-aggressive.

They'll say things like:

- **"You've changed."**
- **"You're too busy now."**
- **"Must be nice."**
- **"You used to be more fun."**

But what they really mean is:

I don't know how to be around you now that you're not in pain anymore.

They liked when you were broken.

They liked when they had more going for them than you did.

They liked being the one who *"had it together."*

They liked when you needed them — when you didn't outgrow them.

But the moment you start growing? Healing? Thriving?

They treat it like betrayal.

Like your glow means you're full of yourself.

Like your healing makes them feel left behind.

They won't admit they're threatened.
Instead, they'll try to humble you.
Through sarcasm.
Through silence.
Through subtle digs that make you feel guilty for evolving.

But here's the truth:
You don't owe anyone your brokenness just to make them feel comfortable.

The Friend Who Wanted Access, Not Accountability

Let's be real:

Not everyone who says **"I love you"** knows how to love you.

And not everyone who wants to be close to you deserves to be.

Some friends don't want connection.

They want *access.*

Access to your energy. Your time. Your loyalty. Your softness.

But try holding them accountable, and suddenly you're **"too much."**

Speak your truth? You're **"starting drama."**

Hold a boundary? You're **"selfish."**

Stop being available 24/7? You're **"not a real friend."**

They want the version of you that bends.

That overgives.

That stays quiet.

That forgives before they even apologize.

But friendship without mutual respect isn't friendship.

It's emotional convenience.

They don't want closeness — they want control.

And they'll twist your words, rewrite the story, and make you the villain

for simply not being their emotional doormat anymore.

And you're allowed to walk the f*ck away from that.

Trauma Bonds Don't Just Happen in Dating

Some of these people? You trauma-bonded with them.
You connected over pain.
Over shared wounds.
Over being misunderstood, underestimated, or rejected.
And that connection felt real — because it *was*.

But shared pain doesn't mean shared values.
Just because someone gets your wounds doesn't mean they'll honor them.
Some friends were only loyal to your brokenness.
Not your growth.
Not your clarity.
Not your boundaries.

You were safe to love when you were still lost.
But the moment you started healing?
They couldn't handle you anymore.
Because healing forced them to look at what they weren't ready to face in themselves.

So they chose distance.
They chose resentment.
They chose to see your growth as betrayal — because they weren't growing too.

That's not your fault.
That's just the truth.

The Slow Burn of Realizing They Don't See You

It doesn't always end in one big fight.

Sometimes it dies slow.

With silence.

With subtweets.

With canceled plans.

With forced smiles and half-hearted replies.

You start noticing things:

- They flake more often
- They stop asking real questions
- They don't celebrate your wins
- They only call when they need something
- They don't notice when you go quiet

And you realize —

You were invested in a friendship with someone who didn't really *see* you.

They saw the version of you that was convenient.

The one who kept the peace.

The one who didn't rock the boat.

The one who showed up no matter how empty she felt inside.

But the version of you who says **"That hurt"**?

Who names what she needs?
Who no longer tolerates breadcrumbs and mixed signals?

They don't know what to do with her.
Because she's no longer easy to control.
She's no longer easy to manipulate.
She's no longer playing the role they picked for her.

Friendship Grief Is Real as F*ck

Nobody talks about the grief that comes with losing a best friend.

There's no breakup playlist.
No sympathy cards.
No one checking in on you three months later.

But the grief?
It hits just as hard.
Sometimes harder.

Because this person saw your soul.
They weren't just part of your life — they were *woven* into it.
They were in your memories. Your healing. Your heartbreak.
They knew your family, your childhood stories, your scars.

You replay memories.
You scroll through screenshots.
You question everything.

And the worst part?
You start wondering if you were the problem.
If maybe you were too sensitive. Too needy. Too intense.

You weren't.
You were just in a friendship that didn't value your *full* self.

Only the version of you they could handle.

That grief is valid.
That heartbreak is real.

That silence you're sitting in?
It's not petty. It's pain.

And just because it wasn't romantic doesn't mean it didn't break you.

The Pressure to Be "Chill" When You're Hurt

You're not weak for caring.
You're not **"dramatic"** for noticing the shift.
You're not **"toxic"** for calling it out.

You're a human with emotions.
And pretending not to have them just to keep the peace is survival, not strength.

You've already spent too much of your life minimizing your own hurt.
Don't do it again just to protect someone else's comfort.

Friendship breakups bring up *deep* sh*t.
Abandonment. Rejection. Family wounds. Trust issues.

It's not just about them leaving.
It's about what that loss awakens inside of you.

So if this cracked something open in you — good.
Let it.

It means you're finally seeing it clearly.
And seeing clearly is the first step to healing.

Why You Held On So Long

You didn't just lose a friend.
You lost what that friendship represented.

A sense of belonging.
A sense of history.
A version of yourself that felt known.

And maybe they were there for you once.
Maybe they held space for you before anyone else did.
Maybe they showed up when the world was crashing down.

But people can be both comforting and harmful.
Both present and manipulative.
Both helpful and toxic.

And that's why it's so confusing.

You miss them.
But you also miss who you were when they still loved you.
Before things got complicated. Before it all went quiet.

But the version of them you're missing?
That was never the *whole* story.

That was the highlight reel.

The part that made it easier to ignore the red flags.
The subtle digs.
The way you were always the one trying harder.
The way your wins felt like losses to them.

You didn't imagine it.
You just finally stopped excusing it.

You're Allowed to Outgrow People

You don't owe anyone a dramatic ending.
You don't need to explain yourself to people who never really saw you.

Sometimes it's quiet.
Sometimes it's just a gut feeling that says, **"I'm done trying."**

You stop texting.
Stop fixing.
Stop justifying.
Stop bending into something smaller than you are.

You're allowed to say:

• **"This friendship doesn't align anymore"**
• **"I care about you, but I can't keep doing this"**
• **"I don't owe anyone access to me just because we've known each other forever"**

Longevity doesn't equal loyalty.
And shared memories don't outweigh your peace.

Final Words for the Ones Who Left When You Got Stronger

To the friend who disappeared the moment I found my voice —
Thank you for showing me who you really were.

To the one who made fun of my healing —
You were never safe.

To the one who loved me broken but couldn't love me whole —
I release you.

To all the friendships that felt like family but left me feeling used —
I'm done twisting myself into a version of me that makes you comfortable.

I may not get closure.
But I get to walk away with my clarity, my voice, and my peace intact.

And that's more than any fake friend ever gave me.
And that's *enough*.

Pause.

Take a moment to be still.
Just breathe.

I DESERVE LOYALTY, TRUTH, AND LOVE.
I RELEASE THOSE WHO NEVER TRULY SAW ME.

Chapter Five

"Just Doing My Job" — Workplace Abuse Dressed as Hustle Culture

Abuse Doesn't End at the Front Door

We talk about toxic relationships.
We talk about dysfunctional families.

But what about the job that drained your *soul*?
What about the boss who weaponized your work ethic?
The coworker who bullied you in the break room?
The leadership team that turned exploitation into a company culture?

Let's talk about that.

Because emotional abuse doesn't clock out at 5pm.
Sometimes, it's built into your **f*cking paycheck.**

And no one warns you about it.
No one tells you how deep it cuts when the place you go to earn a living slowly erodes your sense of self.

You keep showing up.
You keep producing.
You keep trying to prove your value.
While silently crumbling under the weight of expectations that were never *human* to begin with.

And the sickest part?

You get praised for it.

Rewarded for sacrificing your well-being.

Applauded for being the last one to leave and the first one to break.

You're not just tired.

You're exploited.

And you've been conditioned to call it **"a strong work ethic."**

What Workplace Abuse Actually Looks Like

It's not always screaming or harassment in your inbox.
It's not always threats or slurs or lawsuits.

Sometimes, it's the slow erosion of your self-worth while people call it **"just doing your job."**

The red flags are subtle. But they're there:

• Being guilted into skipping breaks
• Being expected to answer messages at all hours
• Being praised for burnout-level effort
• Being ignored when you speak up
• Being micromanaged to the point of losing confidence
• Being excluded from meetings, raises, or recognition
• Being used for your skillset and discarded when you ask for more

They'll call it *dedication.*
They'll call it *professionalism.*
They'll call it being a **"team player."**
They'll shower you with empty praise and public shoutouts while privately draining the life out of you.

But what it actually is: manipulative control, repackaged as work culture.

A system that preys on your fear of being **"difficult," "ungrateful,"** or

"replaceable."

They condition you to equate:

- *Exhaustion* with excellence
- *Silence* with loyalty
- *Burnout* with success

And the second you try to reclaim your boundaries?

You're seen as ungrateful.
Uncooperative.
A problem.

Because their entire system depends on your self-abandonment.

The Boss Who Keeps Moving the Goalpost

You do everything they ask.
Then they ask for more.
You hit the deadline.
They change the expectations.
You speak up.
Suddenly you're **"not a good fit."**

Toxic bosses don't want employees.
They want *puppets.*

They want overachievers with low self-worth and a high tolerance for being disrespected.

They want your grind — not your voice.
Your output — not your boundaries.
Your silence — not your strength.

And when you finally burn out, they'll say, **"You should've said something."**

As if they didn't spend years creating the exact environment that taught you it wasn't safe to speak up.

They played the long game.
They studied your triggers.

They learned how to keep you compliant by dangling **"opportunities"** just far enough out of reach.

You learned the hard way:
• Compliance was rewarded.
• Honesty was punished.
• And the more you gave, the more they expected.

You were never going to win — because the goal wasn't success.
The goal was *obedience*.

And the minute you stopped bowing?
You became disposable.

The Coworker Who Bullies You With a Smile

It's the sarcastic comments in meetings.
The side-eyes.
The jokes made at your expense in front of clients.
The sudden silence when you walk into the room.

And when you finally get the courage to confront it?

They say:
• You're imagining it.
• It was just a joke.
• You're being too sensitive.

It's textbook emotional abuse — disguised as **"office banter."**

And the worst part?
They often get away with it.

Because HR isn't built to protect you.
It's built to protect the company.

So you stay quiet.
You try to rise above it.
You gaslight yourself into believing maybe it *is* all in your head.
Because no one else seems to see it.

But you feel it.
Every day.

In your chest.
In your nervous system.
In the way your heart rate spikes when you see their name on your calendar.
In the way you rehearse conversations in your head before meetings.

That's not professionalism.
That's *trauma.*

And trauma tolerated becomes trauma repeated.

Until eventually, your body starts breaking down in places your mind was too tired to defend.

The Gaslight Called "We're Like a Family Here"

Run.
Run fast.

That line?
That's corporate code for:
We will violate every boundary you have and expect you to thank us for the opportunity.

You're expected to:
• Stay late without compensation
• Be emotionally available for leadership
• Take on the responsibilities of three roles
• Keep your opinions to yourself
• Be loyal even when you're disrespected

And when you finally push back?

They say:
• **"We thought you cared."**
• **"We're disappointed in your attitude."**
• **"We thought you were a team player."**

They flip it on you.
Suddenly you're the one who doesn't care about the team.

Suddenly you're the one being *"negative," "entitled,"* or *"hard to manage."*

F*ck that.

You can care and still have a f*cking limit.
You can give your best and still protect your peace.

Healthy companies don't need to call themselves families.
They show it — through respect, through fairness, through boundaries.

The minute a company asks for your loyalty but won't give you respect,
that's not culture — that's *control.*

Why You Stayed (And Why You Burned Out)

Because you needed the paycheck.
Because you didn't want to be **"the difficult one."**
Because they promised promotions.
Because you were trauma-bonded to being useful.
Because you believed if you just worked hard enough, it would get better.

But no amount of productivity can heal a toxic environment.
No amount of **"keeping your head down"** can protect you from systemic dysfunction.

And no — quitting wasn't weakness.
Burning out wasn't failure.
It was your body trying to save you from something your brain had been conditioned to normalize.

You weren't lazy.
You weren't dramatic.
You weren't ungrateful.

You were surviving.
In a system designed to chew people up and call it *grit*.
In an environment where being drained was considered being driven.

You stayed because it felt safer to suffer than to speak.
And that alone tells you how broken the system is.

The Nervous System Damage Nobody Talks About

Workplace abuse leaves real trauma.

You become:
• Afraid to speak up, even in safe environments
• Hyperaware of tone, body language, silence
• Emotionally exhausted before the day even starts
• Disconnected from your confidence
• Numb in places that used to feel vibrant
• Distrusting of people in leadership — even when they're good
• Guilty for taking breaks or resting

You might find yourself:
• Apologizing constantly
• Over-explaining everything
• Waiting for backlash that never comes — because now you're in a healthier space, but your body hasn't caught up yet

That's what happens when work becomes *survival.*
When you're praised for being selfless while quietly being destroyed.

You don't just leave that behind when you clock out.
You carry it in your muscles.
In your gut.
In your sense of worth.

In the way you second-guess every damn thing you say.

And even after you leave?
There's grief.

Grief for the version of you that tolerated it.
Grief for the passion they killed.
Grief for the career you once loved — before it became a battleground.

The Gaslighting of "Be Grateful You Have a Job"

You tried to speak up.
You tried to express how toxic it felt.
How drained you were.
How impossible it had become.

And someone hit you with the classic:
- **"It's just how this industry is."**
- **"That's corporate life."**
- **"You should be thankful to have this opportunity."**
- **"If you don't like it, leave."**

So you shut up.
You minimized your truth.
You convinced yourself that maybe this is just how it is.

But you know what?
F*ck that.

You are allowed to want respect and a paycheck.
You are allowed to want to feel *safe* at work.
You are allowed to say:

"This is abuse, even if it's happening in an office."

Abuse in a blazer is still abuse.

Manipulation in a meeting is still manipulation.

Exploitation with a salary is still exploitation.

The Aftermath You Carry Home

You didn't just leave work at work.
It followed you.

You snapped at your kids.
You couldn't sleep.
You were too exhausted to enjoy your weekends.
You started questioning if you're even capable anymore.
You lost parts of yourself you haven't even named yet.

You became numb to your own burnout.
Detached from joy.
Too tired to even cry about it.

That's not normal.
That's not sustainable.
That's not your fault.

And no — quitting isn't **"running away."**

It's reclaiming your f*cking sanity.
It's choosing life over performance.
Peace over productivity.
Worth over wage.

It's the bravest thing you've ever done.

And don't let anyone — especially *them* — tell you otherwise.

Final Words for the Places That Broke You

You don't get to have my loyalty anymore.
You don't get to call my trauma a **"learning experience."**
You don't get to spin my burnout as lack of commitment.
You don't get to say I was emotional, when I was actually just **f*cking exhausted.**

I gave you my brilliance.
My time.
My trust.

And you turned it into compliance and called it *culture.*

Never again.

You don't get to define me by the pieces I broke just to keep you happy.

I walked out with my dignity.
And you can keep your toxic praise.

I've finally remembered who the f*ck I am.

And this time — I'm not handing that power over to anyone wearing a name badge.

Pause.

Take a moment to be still.
Just breathe.

My worth is not tied to my productivity.
I protect my energy and my peace.

Chapter Six

Love & Light, My A** — When Healing Spaces Turn Abusive

Not Everyone in a Robe is a Healer

You finally leave the toxic relationship.
You cut off the controlling parent.
You start your healing journey.

You walk into therapy, energy work, reiki, coaching circles, church basements, full moon ceremonies, and online spaces filled with candles, affirmations, and soft-spoken guidance.

And then it happens.

The same manipulation — wrapped in a prettier package.
It doesn't scream this time.
It whispers.

Suddenly you're being told your trauma is a mindset problem.
That your anger is blocking your blessings.
That your boundaries are **"ego."**
That calling out abuse is *"living in the past."*

Welcome to spiritual bypassing.

Where your pain is invalidated with pretty words and smiley emojis.
Where abuse is brushed off with a mantra.
Where accountability is buried under glitter and grace.

And the worst part? You don't even realize it at first.

Because it's packaged in peace.

And you were so desperate for peace, you didn't notice the strings attached.

What Healing Abuse Actually Looks Like

It's not always someone yelling at you.

Sometimes it's a person in a wellness space saying:
- **"Everything happens for a reason"**
- **"You chose this soul lesson"**
- **"Low vibrations attract low experiences"**
- **"You're manifesting this because you're not healed yet"**
- **"Focus on forgiveness, not blame"**
- **"Your trauma is your teacher"**

Sounds peaceful, right?

But what it actually does is this:
- Silences your pain
- Centers blame on the victim
- Protects abusers from accountability
- Turns healing into another system of control

It's gaslighting with a lavender diffuser and a sage bundle.

It's abuse wearing mala beads.

And it's **f*cking dangerous.**

Because you went there to feel safe.

And instead, you were taught to see your suffering as a spiritual flaw.

You went in carrying trauma.
You left carrying shame for even feeling it.

And that is not healing.
That's just trauma with a better marketing team.

The Coach, Therapist, or Healer Who Abused Their Position

You trusted them.
They said they were trauma-informed.
They said they were safe.
They said they were **"here to help."**

And maybe, at first, they were.
They listened.
They held space.
They made you feel seen.

But slowly...
• They crossed boundaries in the name of *"getting to your core"*
• They used their authority to push their agenda
• They spiritualized your suffering instead of validating it
• They made you feel dependent on them
• They criticized your pace, your process, your personality
• They made healing feel like a test you kept failing

You left sessions feeling drained, confused, or ashamed — and still told yourself it was working.
You blamed yourself for not **"surrendering enough."**
You thought maybe your resistance meant they were right.

But they weren't.

They weren't guiding you.
They were feeding their ego off your pain.

And that's not healing.
That's *predatory.*

That's control with a certification.

This is the abuse no one wants to name — because it's hidden in credentials and client testimonials.

But you know how it felt in your gut.
You know how it made you question your own voice.

And that's reason enough to call it what it is.

When Religion Becomes a Weapon

Let's talk about the church.

The spiritual leaders.

The faith communities.

Sometimes the most harmful messages don't come from what they say outright — but from what they shame in silence.

• Telling women to submit no matter what
• Calling abuse **"God testing your strength"**
• Telling people to forgive before they've even felt safe
• Forcing smiles in the name of *"being blessed"*
• Shaming people for being angry
• Teaching trauma as a punishment for disobedience

These messages don't save people.

They *break* them.

They strip them of their autonomy, their voice, their right to feel.

They tell you that obedience is holiness.

That silence is strength.

That enduring pain without question is what makes you faithful.

And when you finally question it?

They call you lost.
They say you're **"turning your back on faith."**

But questioning isn't rebellion.
It's freedom.
It's healing.

It's saying, **"I don't believe in a God who wants me to suffer to be worthy."**
It's saying, **"My pain isn't a sin. It's a signal."**

And it's realizing that sometimes the most spiritual thing you can do — is walk away.

The Red Flags in "Healing" Spaces

Not all healing spaces are safe.
Some are just new containers for the same old dysfunction.

Here's how to know a *"healing"* space is actually toxic — even if it's wrapped in sage and spirituality:
• There's a clear hierarchy or **"guru"** figure
• Boundaries are labeled as ego
• Emotional discomfort is dismissed as **"resistance"**
• You feel like you can't disagree without being labeled **"unhealed"**
• You leave feeling smaller instead of more whole
• You're told your trauma is your fault, even subtly

You may be encouraged to **"take radical responsibility"** for what others did to you.
You may be told your rage is **"low vibration."**
You may be taught that if you haven't forgiven, you're not evolved.

And all of that?
It doesn't heal you.

It shames you.
It polices your pain under the guise of growth.

It turns your journey inward — not to empower you, but to *blame* you.

They say they're just trying to help you *"evolve."*

But what they're really doing is shrinking you into a version of yourself they can control.

Bypassing Isn't Healing

You don't need to **"vibe higher."**
You need to feel safe.
You need to be seen.
You need to grieve, rage, scream, shake, cry, collapse — and not be shamed for any of it.

You don't need someone telling you to forgive.
You need someone to say, **"That should've never happened to you."**
You don't need someone to say, **"Your soul chose this."**
You need someone to say, **"Your humanity didn't deserve it."**

Because healing isn't pretty.
It's not always positive.
It's not always peaceful.

It's messy, painful, sacred reclamation.
It's falling apart.
It's calling sh*t what it is.
It's sobbing in the shower and rebuilding your nervous system one breath at a time.

And any space that tries to bypass that is not a healing space.

It's an echo of abuse.
A prettier prison.

A softer leash.

But a cage nonetheless.

Why You Fell for It (And Why You're Not Stupid)

You were desperate to feel better.
To feel held.
To feel safe.
To feel like something made sense.

And they offered answers.
Comfort.
A system.
A solution.

A place where people used all the right words and promised all the right things.

That doesn't make you naïve.
It makes you *human*.

It means you were brave enough to seek something better.
It means you wanted more than survival.
It means you reached for healing even when you didn't know what it would look like.

And now?

It means you're strong enough to question it.

To walk away.
To call it what it is — even if no one else does.

You didn't fail healing.
You outgrew the bullsh*t.

You realized that any system that shames your humanity in the name of enlightenment is not divine.
It's *manipulative.*

And you're allowed to leave without guilt.

The Difference Between Healing and Harm

Real Healing

- Holds space for anger
- Validates your trauma
- Encourages boundaries
- Honors your pace
- Sees you as whole
- Invites self-trust

Spiritual Bypassing / Healing Abuse

- Labels anger as low vibration
- Minimizes or reinterprets your pain
- Calls boundaries "ego"
- Pressures you to *"just let go"*
- Sees you as broken, needing fixing
- Breeds dependency on them

If the space you're in only works when you stay small, silent, and agreeable — it's not healing.

It's a performance.

And you were never meant to play a supporting role in someone else's idea of enlightenment.

You don't need to be **"more evolved."**
You need to be free.
You need to be sovereign.
You need to be held without being handled.

Guided without being controlled.

Final Words for the Ones Who Dressed Control in Crystals

You said you were helping me.
But you were controlling me.

You spiritualized my pain to avoid facing your own.
You sold me a version of healing that made me feel ashamed of being human.
You preyed on my need to be okay.

And I'm done.

Done being polite.
Done calling it growth when it was actually suppression.
Done playing small so I wouldn't make waves in your calm little container.

You don't get to brand my trauma.
You don't get to repackage my pain and call it purpose.
You don't get to twist my story into a lesson for your audience.

Healing isn't your brand.
It's my birthright.
And I'm taking it back — messy, loud, angry, grieving, glowing, and *whole.*

Exactly as I am.

Exactly as I was always meant to be.

Pause.

Take a moment to be still.

Just breathe.

I DESERVE SAFE SPACES.

I TRUST MY BOUNDARIES AND HONOR MY HEALING JOURNEY.

Chapter Seven

When You Don't Even Recognize Yourself Anymore

This Is the Part No One Prepares You For

You finally leave.

The relationship ends.

The parent is cut off.

The job is done.

The fake friends are blocked.

You did the brave thing.

You walked away.

You survived.

You should feel free.

But instead...

You feel numb.

You feel lost.

You feel disconnected from who you were — and terrified of who you're supposed to be now.

No one tells you that surviving abuse breaks your identity.

Not just your heart.

Not just your trust.

Your **f*cking** sense of self gets shattered.

And you're left standing in the wreckage asking, **"Who the hell even am**

I without them?"

You're not in crisis anymore.
But you're also not okay.
And that's the part that makes you feel like you're failing.

But you're not.

You're just finally in the quiet — and the silence is loud as hell.

The Emotional Hangover After Survival Mode Ends

While you were in it, you were in survival mode.
You didn't have time to feel everything.
You didn't have the luxury of reflection.

You were focused on getting through the day.
Avoiding the next blow-up.
Keeping the peace.
Staying quiet.
Staying safe.

You became a master of reading moods.
Of shrinking your needs.
Of walking on eggshells.
Of *surviving*.

But after it ends?
That's when the waves hit.

• Delayed grief
• Explosive anger
• Shame that shows up out of nowhere
• Flashbacks at the most random times
• Full-on identity collapse
• Emotional confusion that makes you question everything

You're finally **"safe,"** but everything inside you feels unsafe.

Your body still flinches.
Your mind still spirals.
Your heart still races at nothing.

You can't sleep.
You can't breathe without bracing.

That's not weakness.
That's trauma finally catching up.

That's your body saying, **"We held it together for as long as we could."**

The Mirror Becomes a Stranger

You look at pictures and barely recognize the person in them.

She smiled.
She showed up.
She kept it together.

But where the **f*ck** is she now?

You try to do things you used to love and feel nothing.
You try to be social and feel empty.

You question every decision.
You second-guess even your most basic instincts.

You don't even trust your own thoughts.
You don't know what's real anymore.

And you're scared to be alone with yourself — because you don't know who you are without the chaos.

But here's the truth:

You're not being dramatic.
You're not broken.

You're just someone who lost themselves in the fire — and now has to build a new identity from the ashes.

And that's terrifying.
But it's also the beginning.

You're not going backward.
You're just in the middle.

You Start Questioning Everything

• Was any of it real?

• Did I overreact?

• Why did I stay so long?

• Was I actually the toxic one?

• Why do I still miss them?

• Why does healing feel worse than being in it?

These questions feel brutal.

They claw at your chest in the middle of the night.

They haunt you when you're alone.

Because now that you're no longer in fight-or-flight...

your brain has space to start unraveling it all.

This is when the spiral begins.

When your mind starts trying to *figure it all out.*

When you start trying to rewrite the story to make it make sense.

But listen —

You don't have to have the answers.

You don't have to explain it perfectly.

You don't have to know why they did what they did.

You just have to keep choosing yourself — one confusing, messy, shaky

step at a time.

You're allowed to question it all and still keep going.

That's not weakness.

That's healing.

The Grief You Don't Know How to Name

You're grieving things you can't explain.
- The version of you who didn't see it coming
- The innocence you lost
- The years you won't get back
- The people who didn't believe you
- The apologies that never came
- The support that never showed up
- The life you thought you were building that suddenly doesn't exist

And the worst part?
Everyone around you thinks you should be fine now.

You're out.
You're free.
It's "over."

But grief isn't logical.
It doesn't care about timelines.

It doesn't care that the relationship is over or the job is done or the storm has passed.

Grief comes in waves.

It sneaks up in moments you don't expect — in songs, in smells, in memories, in silence.

And some of it isn't even about the people.
It's about the loss of who you thought you were going to be by now.

The Rage That Follows the Silence

You stay quiet for weeks.
Months.
Maybe years.

You minimize.
You internalize.
You pretend it's fine.
You force yourself to be grateful.
You call it growth, even though it feels like suppression.

And then one day — something snaps.

You start feeling angry.
Angry at them.
Angry at the people who stayed silent.
Angry at the world for moving on.
Angry at yourself — for staying, for trusting, for not seeing it sooner.

And then the guilt creeps in.

"Why am I still so mad?"
"Why can't I just move on?"

Because you're finally safe enough to feel it.
Because your body is no longer in survival mode — and now your rage has

room to speak.

Your anger is sacred.
It's not a flaw.
It's a fire that burns away the shame.

It's a voice that says, **"I didn't deserve that. None of it."**

You're allowed to be mad.
You're allowed to let that fire speak.
You're allowed to stop being the **"chill"** version of you that protected everyone else's comfort.

Who Are You Now?

This is the hardest part.
Not the leaving.
Not the ending.

But the becoming.

You don't know what you like anymore.
What you believe.
What your voice sounds like.
What *"normal"* feels like.

You try to rebuild, but it's like putting together a puzzle of a picture you've never seen.
You reach for your old self but find she's gone.

And some days?
You don't even want to rebuild.
You just want to hide.
You want it all to pause so you can breathe.

That doesn't make you weak.
It makes you *real*.

Rebirth doesn't happen in a straight line.
It's not a glow-up.

It's not a milestone you post on Instagram.

It's losing everything you thought you were — and choosing to come back home to yourself anyway.

It's asking:

"Who am I now?" and answering, **"Someone who's figuring it out."**

You Might Still Miss Them

Even after everything.
Even after the abuse.
Even after the betrayal.
Even after the therapy and the truth and the boundaries.

And you'll hate yourself for it.
You'll feel disgusted.
You'll wonder if that means you're still stuck.

But missing someone doesn't mean they were good for you.
It just means there was a part of you that *believed*.
That hoped.
That held on.
That loved.

Don't shame that part.

Hold her.
Thank her.
Tell her she was doing her best with what she knew.

And remind her:

We're not going back.
Not because we hate them — but because we finally love ourselves more.

You're Not Behind — You're Rebuilding

You might feel like you wasted years.
Like you're starting over.
Like everyone else is moving forward while you're standing still in the rubble.

But **f*ck that.**
You're not behind.
You're rebuilding.

And rebuilding takes time.
It's not linear.
It's not shiny.
It's not loud.

It's quiet.
It's painful.
It's sacred.

And the people who are moving fast?
Some of them haven't even realized they're still in cages.
Still in survival mode.
Still performing.
You burned the whole thing down.
And now you get to build something that's real.

That's not failure.

That's **f*cking freedom.**

Final Words for the Version of You Still in the Wreckage

I see you.
Sitting in the dark.
Not knowing who you are.
Wondering if it'll ever feel okay again.
Tired of trying.
Tired of crying.
Tired of fighting for a version of peace that still feels out of reach.

This part of the healing journey is brutal.
But it's also honest.
Sacred.
Necessary.

You are not the broken pieces they left behind.
You are the one who picked them up.
You are the one who survived.
You are the one still standing.

And even if you don't recognize yourself right now,
the real you is in there — waiting.
And she's coming back stronger.

Not because she wants to prove anything.
But because she finally **f*cking can.**

Pause.

Take a moment to be still.
Just breathe.

I AM REDISCOVERING MYSELF EVERY DAY.
MY IDENTITY IS MINE TO RECLAIM.

Chapter Eight

The Isolation, the Shame, and the Silence

This Is the Part They Don't Talk About

You get out.
You cut them off.
You walk away.

And suddenly — it's quiet.

Not peaceful quiet.
Lonely quiet.
The kind of silence that screams.

You thought freedom would feel like exhale.
Like the ending of a horror movie.
Like finally waking up from a nightmare.

But instead, it feels like abandonment.

No more texts.
No more fake apologies.
No more fights.

But also...

No one checking in.
No one saying, **"I believe you."**
No one asking, **"Are you okay?"**

You're alone.

And you're not sure if that's healing — or punishment.

You left hell and expected heaven.
But you landed in *limbo*.

And that in-between space?
It's heavy as **f*ck.**

You start wondering if maybe you were the problem.
Because if you were really the victim, wouldn't someone be here?
Wouldn't someone have stayed?
Wouldn't someone have said, **"I'm proud of you"?**

You start to feel like maybe the silence is saying something.
That maybe your story isn't worth listening to.
That maybe no one cares.

And even worse — maybe they never did.

Where the F*ck Did Everyone Go?

You start noticing the empty space.

People you thought were friends?
Gone.

Family members?
Weirdly neutral.

Support groups?
Full of platitudes and bad advice.

And the people who once said, *"Let me know if you need anything"*?
Never followed up.

You realize how many people only stood by you when you were pretending everything was fine.

They liked the version of you who smiled through the pain.
The one who kept their secrets.
The one who didn't make waves.
The one who performed strength while falling apart inside.

But now that you're speaking up?
Now that you're angry?
Now that you're *naming* it?

They don't know what to do with you.

They avoid your posts.
They change the subject.
They suddenly go quiet.

Turns out, they didn't love you.
They loved the version of you who made them comfortable.

You realize healing doesn't just mean grieving the abuser — it means grieving the people who disappeared when you stopped playing small.

The people who showed up for your *mask* but vanished for your truth.
The ones who liked the idea of your healing journey, but not the actual **f*cking process.**

And god — it hurts.

It hurts in a way you didn't expect.
Like a second betrayal layered on top of the first.
You think you've already lost everything, and then you lose everyone else too.

It's the kind of grief that doesn't come with flowers or casseroles.
It comes with silence.
With ghosted group chats.

With unfollowed accounts.

With people pretending you never existed.

You learn who was real — and who was just rehearsing loyalty until your truth made them uncomfortable.

The Shame Hits Harder Than Expected

You thought once you left, the shame would fade.

But now it's louder than ever.

- How did I let it get that far?
- Why didn't I see the signs?
- Why did I go back?
- Why didn't I tell anyone?
- How could I be so stupid?
- What if no one believes me?

The voice in your head sounds suspiciously like *them*.
The way they used to twist things.
The way they made everything your fault.

Except now?
They're not even here.

And somehow you're still carrying the shame they handed you — blaming yourself for dropping it.

That's how deep it runs.

Even in the quiet, their voice lives inside you.

You start questioning your memories.

Start rewriting the timeline to make it less painful.

Start wondering if you exaggerated the abuse just to justify leaving.

But that shame?

It's not your truth.

It's residue.

It's poison that stayed behind after you walked away.

And every day you wake up and fight to see yourself clearly again — that's healing.

That's strength.

That's resistance in its purest form.

You're not stupid.

You're not broken.

You're healing in a world that teaches you to hate yourself for surviving.

You Don't Tell the Full Story

Not because you're hiding.
But because no one seems ready to hear it.

You try to explain what happened, but people shift in their seats.
They change the subject.
They say,

"But they seemed so nice…"

Or worse,

"You sure you're not being dramatic?"

So you stop talking.
You tell the edited version.
The PG version.
The *"palatable"* version.

And then you go home and sit with the truth alone.

The whole truth.
The parts that made you flinch.
The parts that still make you shake.
The parts that never got to be spoken out loud.

And you wonder — if no one can hold it, does that mean it didn't happen?

But it did.

Even if they can't face it.
Even if they'll never believe it.
Even if you never say it out loud again.

Some truths don't need permission.
They just need space.

And sometimes, the strongest thing you can do is carry your truth — even when the world tries to look away.

This Is What Emotional Isolation Feels Like

You're in a crowded room, but you feel invisible.
You have people around you, but none of them get it.
You post something vulnerable — and it gets ignored.
You try to talk about your pain — and someone says,
"But you're so strong!"

You start to wonder:

Am I too broken to be understood?
Am I too much now?

But no —

You're not broken.
You're just in a part of the healing journey no one knows how to witness.

You're not alone because you're too much.
You're alone because society doesn't know what to do with people who stop pretending.

They want your comeback story.
Not your collapse.

They want resilience.

Not reality.

But real healing?

It's messy.
It's uncomfortable.
And it rarely fits into the inspirational quotes people want to hear.

You weren't meant to go through this alone.
You just learned how to.

You adapted.
You protected your truth by keeping it sacred — even if it cost you connection.

Because not all connection is real.
Some of it was just proximity.
Some of it was just tolerance.
Some of it was just convenient — until you became inconvenient.

The World Moves On — But You're Still Frozen

Time doesn't make sense anymore.

People around you are dating again.
Posting selfies.
Planning vacations.
Getting promotions.
Going to brunch.

And you're still waking up with nightmares.
Still checking the locks three times.
Still flinching at sudden noises.
Still replaying every conversation, wondering if you imagined the whole thing.

You want to be **"normal,"** but you don't even remember what that feels like.

You're not trying to be stuck.
You're trying to survive.
You're trying to feel *real* again.
You're trying to breathe without bracing for impact.

But no one sees it.

Because your pain doesn't bleed in public.

Because you still smile.

Because you still function.

And that's what makes it so easy to miss.

And maybe that's the hardest part — not just surviving the abuse, but surviving the aftermath in a world that never stopped moving.

The Double Life of a Survivor

On the outside:
- You're smiling.
- Working.
- Functioning.

On the inside:
- You're spiraling.
- Grieving.
- Screaming into the void.

This is what surviving abuse looks like *after* the fact.

Not a dramatic breakdown.
A slow, quiet disconnection from yourself.

It's crying in your car and then going into work

— like nothing happened.
It's panic attacks on the bathroom floor

— between parenting or appointments.
It's saying **"I'm good"**

—when you're anything but.

It's pretending you're fine because people stopped asking.

Because you're scared they don't really want the truth.

Because you don't have the energy to explain how it feels to live inside your body now.

And it's **f*cking exhausting.**

You're not failing.
You're surviving a storm that no one else can see.

And you deserve credit for that — even if no one ever gives it to you.

Shame Grows in Silence

You didn't want to become this version of yourself.

The anxious one.
The one who pulls away.
The one who cancels plans.
The one who doesn't respond.
The one who watches people drift away and lets them go — because you're too tired to explain why you're not okay.

But this isn't who you are.
It's who you became to protect yourself.
A version of you that was built in defense mode.
Built to get through.
Built to survive what you weren't meant to survive alone.

And it's okay if you don't have the words yet.
It's okay if healing looks like hiding for a little while.
It's okay if your nervous system needs rest more than reentry.

You don't have to rush back to the world.
You don't have to **"be okay"** for anyone else's comfort.
You don't have to prove you're healing just to be believed.

There's no timeline for coming home to yourself.

There's just patience.

And presence.

And slowly letting the real you take up space again.

You Don't Need to Be Loud to Be Brave

Some survivors speak.
Some write.
Some create art.
Some share their stories online.
And some?

Some stay quiet.

Not because they're ashamed.
But because they're still processing.
Still trying to feel safe in their own skin.
Still figuring out where the pain ends and they begin.

Your silence doesn't mean you're weak.
It means you're listening to your body.
And your body knows what it needs to heal.

Courage isn't always visible.
Bravery doesn't always look like fire.
Sometimes it looks like rest.
Stillness.
Breath.

Not answering the phone.
Not explaining your silence.

Not showing up when you know it'll cost you too much.

Sometimes it looks like being honest with yourself before anyone else.

That's brave as hell.

Final Words for the Ones Still in the Silence

If no one checked on you — this chapter is your check-in.
If no one believed you — this chapter believes you.
If no one saw your pain — this chapter sees it.

You're not crazy.
You're not weak.
You're not behind.
You're not invisible.

You're just in the part of the story where the world went quiet... and your soul started to whisper:

"I'm still here."

And I promise — that whisper becomes a roar.
But for now?

Just breathe.

You made it to the other side.
Now give yourself permission to rest in the truth.

Pause.

Take a moment to be still.
Just breathe.

I AM NOT ALONE.

MY VOICE MATTERS, AND MY HEALING IS VALID.

Chapter Nine

Rage — The Emotion They Told You to Fear

Let's Talk About It — All of It

You tried to be calm.
Reasonable.
Peaceful.
Spiritual.
Soft.

But somewhere beneath the silence
beneath the grief
beneath the shame —

there's **rage.**

And you know what?
It's about **f*cking** time we talk about it.

Because it's not just *okay* to be angry.
It's necessary.

Your rage is not a problem.
It's proof you still know what you deserved.
It's not dysfunction.
It's recognition.

Of every time you stayed quiet to keep the peace.
Of every wound that never got witnessed.

Of every moment you wanted to scream and didn't.

It's the part of you that finally called **bullsh*t**
on all the gaslighting, minimizing, and manipulation.

It's what rises when your nervous system says,
"That was never okay — why did everyone pretend it was?"

Rage is your internal siren
that you ignored for too damn long.

And now it's howling.
And it deserves to be heard.

Not just whispered into your journal.
Not just cried into your pillow.

Loudly.
Sharply.
Fully.

Because that voice you silenced?
That scream you swallowed?
That fire you tucked away?

They were never wrong.
They were right all along.

You were just convinced that peace meant silence.

That survival meant softness.

That love meant never raising your voice — even when you were dying inside.

But love that silences you isn't love.

Peace that erases you isn't peace.

Sometimes rage is the only honest thing left
in a world that taught you how to disappear.

Rage Shows Up When You Stop Lying to Yourself

Rage is what shows up when you finally let yourself tell the truth:

- I didn't deserve that.
- They **f*cked** me up.
- I gave everything and got nothing.
- They lied, gaslit, manipulated, and left me to deal with the wreckage.
- And I'm still the one everyone expects to "take the high road."

You're expected to heal quietly.
To rise gracefully.
To not **"make it worse."**

But inside?
You are burning.

And you *should* be.

You swallowed the storm for too long.
Now it's thundering back through your bones.

You're not exaggerating.
You're not bitter.
You're finally being honest.

This is what it looks like when you stop pretending it didn't hurt.
When you stop romanticizing pain.
When you stop protecting the people who broke you.

Rage doesn't mean you're stuck.
It means you've finally hit the part of your healing
where you no longer accept the bare minimum — even from yourself.

It means you've stopped editing your story
to protect the ones who harmed you.

It means you're not afraid of your truth anymore — even when it makes
people uncomfortable.

It means you're finally siding with yourself.

And that?
That changes everything.

Why Your Rage Makes People Uncomfortable

Because you're not *supposed* to feel this way.

You're supposed to be over it.
Supposed to forgive.
Supposed to **"find the lesson."**
Supposed to be grateful for the growth.

But **f*ck that.**

You're not here to perform peace
for people who never had to survive what you did.

You're not here to water down your truth
so others can swallow it easier.

You're here to stop carrying the weight of what they did in silence.
You're here to stop being the one who makes everyone else comfortable.

And your rage?
That's your body saying,

"No more."

It makes them uncomfortable
because it makes them look in the mirror.

Because it reminds them that you're no longer controllable.
Because it reveals what they tried to pretend never happened.

They don't want to hear your pain.
Because deep down,
they know they stood by and did nothing.

Or worse —
They told you to stay.
To be patient.
To **"try harder."**

Your rage exposes all of it.
The silence.
The complicity.
The convenience.
The cowardice.

And that's why they want you quiet.

Not because you're wrong —
but because your truth ruins their comfort.

They don't want the mirror.
They want the mask.

And you're done wearing it.

This Is Sacred Fire

They called you dramatic when you were finally honest.
They said you were toxic when you set boundaries.
They told you you were unstable when you broke down.

But rage isn't unstable.
It's *clarity.*

It's your nervous system reclaiming power.

It's the part of you that says,
"I deserved better. I should've been safe. That was abuse."

Rage is not hate.
It's self-respect that's been buried under years of gaslighting.

It is holy.
It is primal.
It is yours.

Let that sink in —

The thing they made you fear?
Might just be the thing that finally saves you.

Because that heat inside you?

That's your soul refusing to stay small.

That's your boundaries growing teeth.

That's your intuition lighting a match to everything that tried to cage you.

This isn't dangerous.

This is sacred.

This is fire with a **f*cking purpose.**

You don't have to light the world on fire.

But you do have to stop freezing to keep others warm.

You were never meant to be easy to handle.

You were meant to be whole.

What Rage Feels Like in the Body

Let's name it.

- Jaw tight.
- Hands shaking.
- Chest hot.
- Breath shallow.
- Head pounding.
- Body tense.
- Mind racing with things you should've said.

This is not overreaction.
This is energy that never had a safe place to land.

So you hold it.
You suppress it.
You swallow it.

Until you don't.

Until it breaks through.
Until it demands to be felt.

And when it does?

You feel alive again.

Terrified, yes.

But **f*cking alive.**

That fire you feel?
That's your life force saying,

"I'm still here. And I remember everything."

Your body was never the enemy.
It's been trying to speak for years.

And now it's roaring.

You're not crazy.
You're not overreacting.
You're finally hearing yourself.

And sometimes the loudest healing
starts in your chest.
In your clenched fists.
In the words you've never said out loud.

It's your body testifying
to everything your mouth wasn't allowed to say.

The Truth Is: You Have Every Right to Be Angry

You were lied to.
Used.
Controlled.
Dismissed.
Gaslit.
Abandoned.
Betrayed.

You don't need to explain why you're mad.
You don't need to justify your fury.

You have every right to be enraged at:

• The people who hurt you.
• The ones who stayed silent.
• The systems that protected abusers.
• The years you lost.
• The voice you buried.
• The apologies you never got.

This isn't about holding onto it forever.
This is about finally letting it rise.

Because buried rage doesn't disappear.

It calcifies.

It turns inward.

It becomes shame.

It becomes illness.

It becomes depression.

It becomes self-blame.

Until you set it free.

Until you scream instead of self-destruct.

Until you roar instead of rot.

Your rage is the signal
that you're no longer willing to suffer quietly.

It's the loud declaration:
"This ends with me."

It's the armor you built
out of the fire they thought would destroy you.

Rage Isn't Who You Are — It's What Saved You

You didn't survive by being numb.
You survived by getting mad.

You got sick of the abuse.
Sick of the excuses.
Sick of being the only one trying.
Sick of watching yourself disappear.

And then something snapped.
Something said,

"I'm done."

That wasn't a breakdown.
That was *rebirth*.

You didn't destroy everything.
You refused to be destroyed any longer.

That's not dysfunction.
That's power.

You didn't lose your mind.
You found your limit.

And you honored it — loudly.

Your rage is the boundary
you were never allowed to have before.

It's the scream that says,
"I will not be erased."

It's the moment you became untouchable.
It's the moment the old you died
and the one who knows her worth was born.

The Fear of What Rage Will Do

You might worry:

- What if I say something I regret?
- What if I push people away?
- What if I'm becoming just like them?

But here's the thing:

Rage doesn't make you like them.
Silence did.
Self-abandonment did.
Shrinking yourself to make others comfortable did.

Your rage?
It's not dangerous.

What's dangerous is a woman who's been silenced for too long.

She's the one who burns **sh*t** down and rebuilds something better.
She's the one who says,

"Not one more f*cking time."

You don't need to apologize for that version of you.
She's the one who finally got out.

She's the reason you're alive.

She is not the aftermath.
She is the reason there's a future.

She's the part of you
that will never let you go back.

You Don't Have to Turn It Into Poetry

You don't need to journal it perfectly.
You don't need to make it beautiful.
You don't need to process it publicly.
You don't need to be spiritual about it.

You can punch a pillow.
You can scream in your car.
You can cry and rage and slam your fists on the floor.

This is yours.
You get to feel it messily, fully, honestly.

Because healing isn't all love and light.
Sometimes it's fire and **f*ck this.**

And that is just as sacred.

You don't have to channel it into art.
You don't have to explain it to anyone.
You don't have to clean it up for anyone's comfort.

Stop worrying about how it looks.
Start paying attention to how it *feels*.

That's where the release begins.

That's where the healing starts to breathe.

You're not too much.
You're just finally not shrinking.

And that?
That's what freedom sounds like.
That's what reclaiming your power feels like.

Final Words for the Ones Who Tried to Kill Your Fire

You thought you broke me.
But you awakened something you were never ready for.

You tried to silence me,
but you made me louder.
You tried to make me small,
but you gave me fuel.

I burned quietly for too long.
But now?

I am the flame.
And I will not apologize for the heat.

Let this be the chapter they never saw coming.
Let this be the part where the fire turns to freedom.
Let this be the rage that rebuilds you.

Not the rage that destroys —
but the rage that *reclaims.*
That *resurrects.*
That rises from the ash and says:

"This is mine now."

Pause.

Take a moment to be still.
Just breathe.

My rage is real and righteous.
It fuels my freedom and my boundaries.

Chapter Ten

The Void Between Surviving and Rebuilding

You're Not Drowning Anymore — But You're Not on Land Yet Either

The storm passed.
The chaos stopped.
The abuser is gone.
The toxic people are blocked.
The walls are finally still.

You're not running anymore.
You're not breaking down.
You're not bracing for the next blow.

And yet...

You feel lost as **f*ck.**

You're no longer surviving.
But you don't feel like you're living either.
You're somewhere in between.

Welcome to the void.

The place that no one warned you about.
The part of healing that isn't talked about in the posts with pretty graphics.
The part that doesn't look strong or powerful — just *still.*

Still, heavy, and confusing as hell.

Still unsure if you're healing or just... existing.

Still holding your breath even though the danger is gone.

Because no one tells you that peace comes slowly — and sometimes, it feels more like grief than relief.

No one tells you that sometimes, peace feels like loneliness.

That silence, after trauma, can feel louder than the screams.

That safety might not feel comforting at first — it might feel foreign.

What the Void Feels Like

It's the space between pain and peace.
The silence after survival.
The emptiness that comes when the noise stops — but nothing has filled the space you cleared.

It's not loud.
It's not dramatic.
It's not full of breakthroughs.
It's just... *blank*.

You're:

• Numb.
• Detached.
• Exhausted.
• Questioning everything.
• Feeling like you should be farther than you are.
• Trying to be grateful but still grieving.
• Alive but disconnected.

You wake up and stare at the ceiling, wondering what the point is.
You go through the motions because that's all you know.

You function — but you don't *feel*.
You smile — but it doesn't reach your eyes.

You check off the boxes — eat, shower, respond, sleep.
But none of it feels real.

You're playing a role you don't remember auditioning for.

Everything feels mechanical.
Autopilot.

You laugh at a show, but there's no real spark.
You hug your child, and the love is there — but the numbness is too.

You keep thinking,
"Shouldn't I feel better by now?"
"Shouldn't this be over?"
But healing doesn't move like that.

It doesn't go:
pain → breakthrough → peace.

Sometimes it goes:
pain → survival → collapse → silence → floating → rebuilding.

This?
This is the floating part.
The in-between.

The part where your soul is still catching up with everything you just survived.

You're not sinking.
You're not soaring.

You're just suspended — in between two versions of yourself.

You're no longer who you were — but not quite who you're becoming either.

It's disorienting.
It's lonely.
It's necessary.

And while you might not feel powerful here — this part is where power begins.

You Feel Unmotivated, But It's Not Laziness

You have no energy.
No drive.
No vision.

You try to journal and nothing comes.
You try to create and everything feels forced.
You try to make decisions and second-guess every one.

Your brain feels foggy.
Your body feels heavy.
Your thoughts feel flat.

You're not lazy.
You're not broken.

You're just emotionally and spiritually exhausted.

The fight may be over — but your nervous system still thinks it's at war.
Still waiting.
Still on edge.
Still responding to a threat that's no longer there.

This isn't regression.
This is *recalibration*.

This is your body saying, **"I need a f*cking minute."**

Let your body catch up.
Let your soul catch its breath.

Because when you've been in survival mode for that long, stillness doesn't feel natural.
Rest feels unsafe.
Slowness feels like failure.

But none of that is true.

You're not lazy for not having the energy to push.
You're healing in ways that can't be measured.

Even when the outside looks still — your insides are sorting through a lifetime of pain.

Even when you're doing nothing, you're undoing everything they convinced you to be.

Even when you sit on the couch doing nothing, you're practicing presence — something that was stolen from you for years.

You Don't Trust the Calm

You wait for the next hit.
The next betrayal.
The next rug to be pulled out.

You want peace — but you don't believe in it yet.

You're suspicious of calm.
Uncomfortable with joy.
Uneasy with stillness.

Because calm used to come right before the chaos.
Before the screaming.
Before the gaslighting.
Before the heartbreak.

So now, when everything goes quiet — your heart races.
Your thoughts spiral.
Your body braces.

You flinch at kindness.
You analyze silence.
You brace for the loss that hasn't come yet.

But now?

There's no chaos coming.
No blow-up on the horizon.
No mask slipping off.

Your system just doesn't know that yet.

You're detoxing from fear.
From crisis.
From adrenaline.

And detox doesn't always look like healing.

It looks like discomfort.
Like confusion.
Like fear without a source.

But eventually —

Your body will stop flinching at silence.
Your mind will stop panicking in peace.

And you'll begin to believe in calm again.

You'll stop mistaking safety for boredom.
You'll stop interpreting ease as danger.

You'll learn that peace doesn't mean **"nothing's coming"** — it means you're finally allowed to stay.

It means you're finally allowed to rest without consequence.
To feel without fear.
To exist without apology.

The Void Is Quiet, But It's Not Empty

You feel like you're in limbo.
But something is happening.

Under the surface:
Your nervous system is healing.
Your mind is slowly untangling the lies.
Your energy is recalibrating.
Your identity is rewriting itself.

This isn't nothing.
It just feels like nothing because you're used to noise, stress, and survival.

But real healing is quiet.
It happens in the spaces where nothing seems to be moving — but everything is shifting.

It's slow.
Invisible.
Found in the tiniest of moments.

Like when you say no and don't feel guilty.
When you finally rest without apologizing.
When your body no longer expects pain in stillness.

I remember hitting a place so dark, I didn't even recognize my own thoughts.

I reached out to people — friends, people I trusted — and no one answered.

I just sat there.
Numb.
Not crying.
Not thinking.
Just *done.*

The next morning, I got the kids ready for school like nothing happened.

That kind of silence changes you.

Not because it destroys you — but because it forces you to meet yourself in the quiet.
It's where you learn that the only person who's going to save you — is you.

And even in the stillness, your body remembers what it survived.
Your soul knows what it took to get here.

And you begin to rebuild — not loudly, but steadily.
You begin to hear yourself again.
You begin to trust that voice.

And slowly — without knowing exactly how — you begin to come back to life.

You Start Wanting More — and Then Feel Guilty for It

You feel selfish for wanting happiness.
You feel guilty for laughing.
You feel uncomfortable even thinking about joy.

You start craving things — love, joy, connection — but you don't trust yourself to choose right.

You remember what happened last time.
You remember how being hopeful made you vulnerable.
How wanting something good backfired.
How trusting someone only led to disappointment.

Wanting more after abuse feels dangerous.
Because your mind still links desire with danger.
Hope with betrayal.
Connection with pain.

But this is also a sign:

You're ready for more.

Even if it terrifies you.
Even if you don't feel **"ready."**
Even if part of you still doesn't believe you deserve it.

This is growth.

Real, scary, unglamorous growth.

You're not wrong for wanting love that doesn't hurt.
Or peace that doesn't disappear.
Or a life that feels soft and steady.

That longing?
It's not weakness.
It's the return of your spirit.
It's your soul remembering what it's meant for.

And even if you don't fully believe it yet — you're still allowed to want more.

You're still allowed to dream.

You Know This Part If…

• You're scared of resting because you don't know what will come up when you do.

• You finally have peace, but can't relax into it.

• You cry over things you thought you already healed.

• You want to move forward, but everything feels stuck.

• You're exhausted by doing nothing — and even more exhausted by doing anything.

• You miss the people who hurt you, and you hate yourself for it.

• You replay everything, trying to make it make sense — even though it never will.

• You crave closeness but pull away the second someone gets too close.

• You wonder if maybe you're just not meant for happiness.

• You feel too broken to belong — even though you're not.

• You feel your inner voice coming back — but it still sounds unsure.

• You don't know where you're going next — but you know you can't go back.

The Void Isn't a Setback — It's a Threshold

It feels like nothing.
But it's actually *everything*.

It's the space between who you were and who you're becoming.

It's where the old patterns die.
Where your nervous system learns to relax.
Where your soul starts whispering again — after years of being drowned out by fear.

It's where your body finally slows down.
Where you pause long enough to hear your own voice again.
Where your intuition gets louder than your triggers.

You don't build from survival.
You build from here.

This is the part no one claps for —
but it's the most powerful part of all.

Because this is the part where you rise — not loudly.
Not dramatically.
But quietly, from within.

You stop waiting to be chosen.

You stop proving your worth.

You stop begging for peace — because you've already paid for it in pain.

This is where you remember who you were — before they broke you.

And start choosing who you'll be now — from your own truth.

If You're Floating Right Now…

You don't need a five-year plan.
You don't need to **"figure it out."**
You don't need to rush into your next chapter.

You just need to:

• Sleep.
• Cry.
• Drink water.
• Say no.
• Breathe.
• Move your body.
• Turn off your phone.
• Light a candle.
• Sit in the sun.
• Be soft with yourself.
• Take one honest breath at a time.

This is integration.

This is real healing.

And it doesn't look like much from the outside —
but it's changing you.

It's where you finally stop surviving... and start *becoming*.

You're not lost.
You're *re-forming*.

Piece by f*cking piece.

The healing might be quiet — but your return will be loud.

Final Words for the Ones in the In-Between

You're not doing anything wrong.
You're not broken for not being **"better"** yet.
You're not falling behind.
You're not wasting time.

You're just in the void.

And the void isn't your enemy.
It's your resting place.
It's your rebirth space.
It's the pause before the rebuild.

Don't rush this part.
Don't numb it.
Don't shame it.

Because on the other side of it?
Is the version of you who doesn't settle.
Who doesn't shrink.
Who doesn't chase people to feel worthy.

On the other side is the you who walks away from chaos — without explaining herself.

Who doesn't need permission to take up space.
Who trusts her own voice more than anyone else's.
Who never abandons herself again.

Pause.

Take a moment to be still.
Just breathe.

I HONOR MY PACE.

I HOLD SPACE FOR BOTH PAIN AND GROWTH.

Chapter Eleven

Coming Back Home to Yourself

The Moment You Realize You're Still Here

It doesn't start with fireworks.
It starts with one small moment.

You laugh — and it feels *real.*
You look in the mirror — and don't flinch.
You say **"no"** — and don't feel guilty.

You breathe deeper.
You sleep a little easier.
You wake up without dread.

And for the first time in what feels like forever — you feel like you're coming *home.*

Not to a place.
To yourself.

It's quiet.
Not the scary kind.
Not the silence that used to scream.

But a stillness that finally feels safe.

You sit with yourself... and you don't want to run.
You don't want to numb.

You don't want to distract.

That moment?
That's when you know — you survived it.

All of it.

And something inside you is finally shifting.

It doesn't mean the pain is gone.
It means you're finally more *you* than the pain ever was.

It means you're no longer trying to outrun your past — you're just walking toward your future.

It means you're not waiting to be rescued anymore.
You're not hoping for someone to finally understand.

You've realized the person you needed all along... was *you*.

And that changes everything.

It's Not a Glow-Up. It's a Reclamation.

This isn't about becoming a new person.
It's about remembering the version of you they tried to erase.

The one who trusted her gut.
The one who felt deeply.
The one who dreamed big.
The one who didn't apologize for existing.
The one who used to speak without shrinking.
The one who didn't carry the weight of everyone else's emotions.
The one who didn't second-guess every move out of fear of being *"too much."*

You're not reinventing.
You're *returning*.

And yeah, she's different now.

Stronger.
Softer.
Sharper.

Not naive.
Not bitter.

But aware.

Awake.
Untouchable in a way she never was before.

Because now? You know what it cost to lose yourself — and you're not paying that price again.

This isn't about makeup or milestones or performing *"healed."*
It's about the unshakable knowing that you belong to yourself again.

That your soul is no longer up for negotiation.
That your heart is no longer a battlefield for people who never earned it.

You're not here to prove your transformation.
You're here to live it.

You're here to reclaim the parts of you that felt too sensitive, too intuitive, too soft for this world — only to realize they were your power all along.

You didn't outgrow yourself.
You grew into your *truth*.

You stopped pretending your depth was a flaw.
You started honoring your sensitivity as sacred.

You Start Noticing What No Longer Fits

You're not forcing friendships that feel fake.
You're not laughing at **sh*t** that makes you uncomfortable.
You're not saying *"it's fine"* when it's not.
You're not keeping quiet to make others more comfortable.

You're walking through the same world, but nothing feels the same.
Because you're not the same.

And that changes *everything*.

You can't unsee the truth.
You can't unfeel what healing gave you.
You can't unknow what peace actually costs.

So you let go.

Not with drama.
Not with rage.

With *clarity*.
With *choice*.
With boundaries that don't need explanations.

And that kind of letting go?
That's the most dangerous kind — because it doesn't scream.

It doesn't justify.

It just... happens.

Because you finally know you deserve better.

You don't explain it.
You don't defend it.
You just leave what no longer honors you.

And it feels like *freedom.*
It feels like *truth.*
It feels like finally exhaling after holding your breath for years.

You stop mourning the loss of what was never meant for you.
You stop holding space for people who never held space for you.
You stop confusing guilt with loyalty.
You stop letting *"history"* be a reason to keep someone in your life who continues to write pain into your present.

And just because something used to feel like home doesn't mean it still does.

Sometimes peace looks like walking away — even when the past begs you to stay.

You Relearn What Safety Feels Like

You stop mistaking anxiety for connection.

You stop chasing chaos because it feels familiar.

You stop performing emotional CPR on people who never gave a sh*t about your oxygen.

You start asking:

- Does my body feel calm around them?
- Can I breathe in this space?
- Is this real, or is this survival pretending to be love?
- Is my nervous system relaxed, or just distracted?
- Am I being seen — or just tolerated?

You stop explaining away red flags.

You stop talking yourself into relationships that drain you.

You stop betraying yourself just to be chosen.

Because now you know — peace is the new non-negotiable.

Not silence.

Not passivity.

Not fake positivity.

Peace.

The kind that doesn't cost your voice, your energy, or your identity.

You don't beg for it.
You *build* it.

And you don't let anyone jeopardize it — no matter how close they once were.
You protect it like the sacred thing it is.

Because you remember what it felt like to live without it — and you're never going back to that version of you again.

You've seen what happens when you sacrifice yourself just to avoid conflict.
You've lived the consequences of peace that was performative — peace that depended on your silence.

Now?

Your safety starts within.

And it doesn't ask for permission anymore.
It walks into the room and takes up space.
It chooses rest over rushing.
It chooses stillness over proving.
It chooses *you* — every single time.

You Create a Life That Matches the Truth You Finally Own

You start making changes.

Small ones, at first:

• Saying **"no"** and not explaining.
• Deleting numbers without warning.
• Blocking people without guilt.
• Only answering calls when you have energy.
• Dressing for *you*, not them.
• Saying what you **f*cking** mean.

You stop rearranging yourself to be digestible.
You stop bending until you break.
You stop making yourself small just to be invited.

Then the bigger shifts come:

• You change your circle.
• You change your schedule.
• You change the way you speak to yourself.
• You stop living for survival and start living from *center*.
• You stop waiting for the next breakdown and start building a foundation.
• You don't just heal — you rebuild.

• You don't just cope — you create.

This is what coming home looks like:

Your external life starts matching your internal truth.
You're no longer performing the version of you the world preferred.
You're embodying the version of you that feels true.

And that alignment?
It feels like breathing for the first time in years.

It feels like *truth*, like *power*, like *wholeness*.

Not everyone will recognize you.
Some will miss the version of you who overextended, over-explained, and over-apologized.

But you won't miss her.

Because you finally remember who you are without the wounds running the show.

You stopped watering dead things.
You started growing roots.

You stopped chasing peace — and started becoming it.

You Hold Space for the Whole You — Not Just the "Healed" Parts

You stop being at war with yourself.

You stop criticizing your pain.

You stop editing your emotions to make them palatable for others.

You make room for:

• The triggered version.

• The angry version.

• The exhausted version.

• The anxious version.

• The awkward, loud, messy, passionate, grieving, complicated, *wildly human* version.

You don't abandon her anymore.

You hold her.

You listen to her.

You stop silencing her just to make other people comfortable.

You realize that healing isn't about perfection.

It's about *wholeness.*

You are allowed to be radiant and wrecked.

Joyful and tender.

Empowered and still unraveling.

You are not a contradiction — you are a masterpiece of survival.

That's the revolution.

Being loyal to yourself.
Not just when you're strong — but when you're scared.
When you're spiraling.
When you're healing at a snail's pace.

You stay.
You don't abandon.
You don't shame.

You just stay.

And that changes everything.

You become the love you always needed.
The safety you never had.
The voice that says, **"You're still worthy — even like this."**

Because you're not here to be polished.
You're here to be *whole*.

And whole means holding all of you — especially the parts that once went unseen.

Especially the parts that once made others uncomfortable.
Especially the parts that still feel fragile.

Even the ones you were told to hide.

You Don't Beg to Be Chosen — You Choose Yourself

You don't chase anymore.
You attract.
You align.
You anchor.

You don't beg for love.
You *become* love.
You don't shrink to fit.
You expand.
You don't prove your worth.
You protect it.
You don't wait for someone to come save you.
You save yourself.

And what a **f*cking** plot twist that is.

Because they expected you to stay broken.
To stay small.
To stay silent.
To stay doubting yourself.

But instead?

You *rose.*

Not for them.
Not to prove a point.

For *you.*

Because *you are the point.*

You don't wait to be chosen anymore.
You choose yourself every damn day.

And you know now — that's more than enough.

You love yourself in ways they never could.
You show up for yourself in ways they never did.

You stopped settling for crumbs — and started demanding a feast you built on your own damn table.

You became your own damn miracle.

Final Words for the Version of You Who Thought She'd Never Come Back

Look at you.

Still here.
Still breathing.
Still feeling.
Still trying.

You thought you'd never get out.
Never feel anything good again.
Never trust.
Never hope.
Never believe in yourself again.

And yet — here you are.

Not perfect.
Not fully healed.
Not finished.

But **f*cking home.**

And that's everything.

So if no one has told you lately —

I'm proud of you.

For waking up when you wanted to disappear.
For loving even when it hurt.
For rebuilding with pieces you never asked to hold.
For showing up for yourself — over and over — when no one else did.

You didn't just survive.
You *came back.*

And this time?

You're not leaving yourself behind again.
You're not dimming.
You're not folding.
You're not apologizing for who you've become.

You are *home.*
You are *whole.*
You are *free.*

And **f*ck,** you earned this.

Don't ever forget that.
Not when it's hard.
Not when you doubt yourself.

Not when old wounds whisper lies.

This version of you?

She's the truth.

Pause.

Take a moment to be still.
Just breathe.

I AM COMING HOME TO ME.
I AM SAFE IN MY OWN SKIN.

Chapter Twelve

Rebuilding Without Losing Yourself Again

The World Wants You to Rush This Part

As soon as you start looking okay again — people expect you to move on.

Be productive.
Bounce back.
Start over.

They ask if you're *"over it"* before you've even finished grieving.
They cheer for your glow-up before your nervous system feels safe.
They want your comeback story wrapped in a neat little bow — not the mess it takes to rebuild a life from scratch.

But they don't see what rebuilding actually looks like.

They don't see the fear in every decision.
The grief in every goodbye.
The hesitation behind every *"yes."*
The second-guessing.
The body flashbacks.
The moments when you're frozen in front of a sink full of dishes — because everything feels too loud.
Because the thought of doing one more thing feels like it might crush you.
Because your brain is screaming, but your face is smiling.
Because you're not ready — but you don't want to let anyone down.
Because you're scared to feel safe again.

They don't see the hours spent overthinking one text.

Or the way your body still reacts to a memory from five years ago.

They don't see you flinch when the tone shifts in a conversation.

Or the way your hands shake when you hear your phone go off.

They don't see you reliving old fights in your head just to figure out what you did wrong.

They don't see you sitting alone on the bathroom floor — *again* — wondering how you'll keep going.

Because rebuilding after abuse doesn't start with fresh paint or a new relationship.

It starts with small, quiet, brutal moments.

Saying **"I don't deserve that"** out loud even when your voice shakes.

Reminding yourself *"this isn't my fault"* on repeat until it starts to stick.

Noticing what makes your stomach twist — and actually choosing not to ignore it this time.

It starts with trusting yourself.

Again.

Slowly.

Reluctantly.

But still — you try.

It starts with boundaries.

With grief.

With getting real about what was never okay.

It starts when you stop making excuses for them.

And start making space for yourself.

Rebuilding means accepting the cracks.

The pieces you still don't know how to fix.

The habits you wish you didn't have.

The anger you're afraid to feel.

The softness you're scared to show.

It means moving forward even when your legs shake.

Even when your voice cracks.

Even when your whole body tells you to shut down.

Because you're no longer living to survive.

You're learning to live from *truth*.

You're finally understanding that healing isn't about being fearless — it's about moving forward while fear still lingers in the background.

You're Not Rebuilding What Was — You're Building What Never Was

Let's be clear:

You're not trying to get *"back"* to who you were.
You're not chasing old versions of yourself.
You're not recreating the life that burned down.

Because the truth is — that life was built on trauma.
On survival.
On self-abandonment.
On shrinking.
On performing.
On being easy to love... even when it destroyed you.

You were functioning — barely.
But calling it *"normal."*
Smiling on cue.
Saying *"I'm fine"* when you were disassociating every day.
Making jokes to distract from the pain.
Being the peacekeeper, the fixer, the forgiver — so you didn't get punished.

So no — you're not going back.
You're going *forward*.

You're building a life from truth this time.

From peace.

From alignment.

From your *gut* — not your guilt.

And that kind of life?

It takes time.

It takes work.

It takes ruthless self-honesty.

It takes saying, *"This doesn't work for me anymore,"* even when people don't understand.

It takes disappointing others to finally stop disappointing yourself.

It takes letting go of people who never saw the real you.

It takes grieving the version of you that tolerated it all.

And it's worth every painful, beautiful, raw step.

Because for the first time — you're building something that feels like *you*.

Not the *"you"* they told you to be.

Not the *"you"* you had to become to survive.

But the you who finally feels safe to show up.

This Time, You Build With Boundaries

No more overexplaining.
No more guilt when you say no.
No more second chances for people who showed you who they are.
No more keeping people around because *"they mean well."*

This version of you?
She protects her energy like it's sacred — because *it is.*

She doesn't hand it out to people who haven't earned it.
She knows that love without safety isn't love at all.
She doesn't play tug-of-war with people who only come close to pull her back in.

You've learned:

• Boundaries aren't walls.
• Boundaries are doors that you open on purpose.
• Boundaries don't make you rude.
• Boundaries make you *real.*
• Boundaries aren't about controlling others — they're about honoring yourself.

And the people who respect them?

Those are your people.

The ones who don't need to be convinced.

The ones who hear *"no"* and don't take it as rejection.

The ones who make room for your healing without making it about them.

Not the ones who push.

Not the ones who guilt-trip you.

Not the ones who say *"You've changed"* when you stop tolerating their **bullsh*t.**

You don't defend your peace anymore.

You just don't let them in.

And you're not sorry about it.

You Don't Let Potential Trick You This Time

You're done falling for *"what could be."*

You don't date red flags just because they come with pretty words.

You don't stay just because they say they're *"working on it."*

You don't make excuses for inconsistent behavior.

This time, you watch what *is*.

You listen to patterns.

Not apologies.

You track actions.

Not words.

You observe how you feel in someone's presence — and if your body says *"no,"* you honor it.

Even if you still love them.
Even if they *"didn't mean to."*
Even if it's complicated.

Because you've already seen what happens when you ignore your gut.
You know what it costs.

Now?

Your intuition is your compass.
Your body is your barometer.
And your peace is your litmus test.

You're not getting lost again.

Not for love.
Not for loyalty.
Not for the version of someone they promised they'd become.

You finally trust yourself more than the fantasy.

And that's everything.

The Little Things Mean More Now

You start noticing joy in the small things:

- A cup of coffee in silence.
- A belly laugh that comes out of nowhere.
- A playlist that makes you feel powerful again.
- A deep breath that doesn't feel heavy.
- An afternoon with no triggers.
- A conversation that doesn't drain you.
- A clean kitchen that makes you feel calm.
- A text from someone who doesn't expect anything in return.
- A night where your mind didn't spiral.
- A moment where you didn't brace for the worst.
- A full-body exhale that didn't feel forced.
- A morning where your first thought wasn't panic.

This is what rebuilding actually looks like.

It's not big wins.
It's not overnight healing.

It's micro-moments of safety, joy, softness, and clarity that remind you:

I'm not in survival anymore.

You're still cautious.

Still tender.
Still healing.

But you're here.

And that's everything.

You Redefine Success

You used to chase perfection.
Now you chase *peace.*

You used to measure your worth by what you did.
Now you measure it by how you *feel.*

You stop asking:

- *"Am I productive?"*
- *"Do they approve of me?"*
- *"Am I doing enough?"*

And start asking:

- *"Does this align?"*
- *"Am I betraying myself right now?"*
- *"Is this real, or is this performance?"*
- *"Would I still say yes if no one clapped for it?"*

You realize that success isn't achievement.
It's *authenticity.*

It's freedom.
It's knowing who you are — and refusing to abandon her for validation
ever again.

You Get Clear on What You'll Never Tolerate Again

This is when the list starts forming — quietly, but fiercely.

You don't need to shout it from the rooftops.
You just start *living* it.

You decide:

- I will never ignore my gut to avoid conflict again.
- I will never water myself down to be loved.
- I will never confuse chaos with connection.
- I will never explain my worth to someone who doesn't see it.
- I will never carry shame for how I survived.
- I will never silence myself just to be understood.
- I will never abandon myself to make someone else comfortable.
- I will never let anyone guilt me into staying small.
- I will never be the only one trying.
- I will never trade my peace for temporary attention.
- I will never pretend I'm okay just to make others feel better.
- I will never again see red flags and call it *growth*.

These aren't walls.

These are *standards*.

And they're rooted in self-respect.

Not arrogance.
Not ego.

Self-respect.

And that kind of clarity?

It doesn't just change your relationships.
It changes your *entire life.*

You Choose Yourself — Over and Over Again

This time, you don't lose yourself in the process.
You don't contort yourself to be chosen.
You don't twist your truth to avoid being alone.

This time, when red flags show up — you leave.
When your nervous system speaks — you listen.
When your needs feel *"too much"* — you meet them anyway.

You don't beg.
You don't chase.
You don't pretend.

Because now, you know:

If the cost of connection is abandoning yourself — it's not connection.
It's *self-betrayal.*

And you're done with that.

You're not just rebuilding a life.
You're rebuilding *yourself* — with honesty, intention, boundaries, and
f*cking grace.

Final Words for the Rebuilder

You're doing it.

Quietly.
Gently.
Radically.

You're making decisions that align.
You're turning down energy that doesn't.
You're putting yourself first without apologizing.
You're listening when your soul says *"not this."*
You're catching the spiral before it swallows you.
You're saying *"I need rest"* and not feeling guilty for it.
You're noticing what drains you — and choosing not to go.
You're protecting your peace like it's the most valuable thing you own —
because *it is.*

You're rewriting the story — one boundary, one breath, one brave choice
at a time

You're not just surviving anymore.

You're building a life that reflects your healing.

And whether anyone claps for it or not — you should be **f*cking proud.**

Because this isn't easy.

This isn't fast.

This isn't flashy.

This is *sacred* work.

And no one can take it from you.

Pause.

Take a moment to be still.
Just breathe.

I BUILD FROM TRUTH, NOT GUILT.
I AM WHOLE EVEN IN THE CRACKS.

Chapter Thirteen

Real Love Doesn't Hurt Like That

You Thought It Was Love — But It Wasn't

They said they loved you.
And you believed them.
Why wouldn't you?

They called you beautiful.
Held you when you cried.
Told you they'd never leave.
Maybe they even talked about forever.

But here's the thing:

Real love doesn't make you question your worth.
Real love doesn't gaslight you.
Real love doesn't punish your honesty.
Real love doesn't make you beg to be seen.

It doesn't shatter your sense of self and then tell you you're *"too sensitive."*
It doesn't say *"I love you"* with one hand and destroy you with the other.

That wasn't love.
That was **control** dressed in affection.
Manipulation wrapped in romance.
Power games hiding behind *connection.*

And I know that's hard to hear.

Because you wanted it to be real.

You gave it your all.

You meant it.

But just because you loved them doesn't mean they were capable of loving you back in a healthy way.

Real love doesn't leave you doubting yourself.

It doesn't chip away at your spirit until you don't recognize your own reflection.

It doesn't turn your kindness into a weapon and call it love.

It builds — it doesn't destroy.

It brings clarity — not confusion.

And it never asks you to prove your worth.

Love Bombs Are Not Love

They came on strong.
The connection was *instant.*
The chemistry intense.
The compliments nonstop.
They talked about soulmates, fate, forever — fast.

It felt like a dream.

But **real love doesn't overwhelm your nervous system.**
It doesn't flood you and then drain you.
It doesn't pull you close just to push you away.
It doesn't love you loud in public and ignore you in private.
It doesn't leave you confused, anxious, or doubting your reality.

You weren't being swept off your feet.
You were being **disarmed.**

Love bombing isn't passion.
It's **manipulation.**
It's **grooming.**
It's a calculated effort to earn your trust — so they can violate it later.

And once you've felt *safe* love, you'll feel the difference immediately.
Your body will know.

Because **safe love doesn't feel like chaos.**

It feels like peace.

And if that feels foreign — it's not because something's wrong with the love.

It's because something happened to you.

It's because your nervous system is wired for survival, not softness.

It's because your definition of love was shaped by trauma.

But just because pain was your baseline doesn't mean it has to stay that way.

You get to rewrite the blueprint.

You get to unlearn the belief that love has to hurt to be real.

Real Love Doesn't Make You Prove Your Pain

In trauma, you're used to being doubted.
Disbelieved.
Dismissed.

You're used to repeating yourself.
Explaining your tone.
Justifying your triggers.
Defending your truth.

You're used to people saying:
- *"Why are you still upset?"*
- *"That didn't happen."*
- *"You're too much."*
- *"You're overreacting."*

But **real love?**
Believes you.

You don't have to perform your trauma to be supported.
You don't have to explain every scar to be held.
You don't have to shrink to keep the peace.
You don't have to educate someone just to be understood.

You get to exist — in all your complexity — and they stay.

That's love.

Not performance.
Not pressure.
Not convincing someone to care.

Just presence.
Compassion.
Listening.
Respect.

Real love leans in when you flinch.
It doesn't retreat when you cry.
It doesn't ask you to hurry up and be healed.

It holds space for the broken pieces without trying to fix or flee.
It accepts the past you carry — without making it your burden to justify.

Real Love Holds Space for All of You

Not just the healed parts.
Not just the calm days.
Not just the moments when you're easy to love.

Real love says:
- *"Tell me what you're scared of. I want to understand."*
- *"You don't have to pretend with me."*
- *"I'm not leaving when it gets hard."*

It doesn't call you crazy for having triggers.
It doesn't punish you for needing reassurance.
It doesn't shame you for moving slow.
It doesn't twist your vulnerability into a weapon.

Real love doesn't take your trauma personally.
It makes space for it.

Not because it's their responsibility to fix it — but because they care enough to witness it without flinching.

Real love meets you where you are — without demanding you skip steps to be palatable.

You don't have to wear a mask.
You don't have to shrink your emotions to be palatable.

You get to be fully human — messy, healing, complicated.
And still loved.

Even when you don't know how to ask for what you need.
Even when you shut down.
Even when the past screams louder than the present.

They don't walk on eggshells — they walk beside you.
They don't demand the *"best version"* of you.
They honor every version.

Real Love Feels Safe in the Body

Your trauma taught you that love = chaos.
That if your heart isn't racing, it must not be real.
That if there's no high, there's no connection.

You learned to associate adrenaline with affection.
You confused anxiety with excitement.
You mistook obsession for chemistry.

But your body knows.

Even if your mind still questions it.

Real love feels like:
• Calm.
• Softness.
• Steadiness.
• Laughter that isn't followed by a breakdown.
• A nervous system that doesn't feel like it's in danger.
• Quiet mornings that don't make you brace.
• Conversations that don't make you spiral afterward.

You don't feel obsessed.
You feel *held.*
You don't feel addicted.
You feel *supported.*

And yes — it might feel boring at first.
But that's only because peace feels foreign when you've lived in survival.

Boring isn't bad.
It's just unfamiliar.
Your system is adjusting.

And that's not a red flag.
That's a **f*cking miracle.**

It's safety.
It's consistency.
It's the opposite of the emotional rollercoaster you *thought* was love.

And it might scare you at first — because it asks nothing of you except to
be.
It doesn't demand performance.
It invites *presence.*

You Don't Have to Earn It This Time

Real love doesn't make you hustle for it.

It doesn't make you guess.
It doesn't keep you in limbo.

You don't have to prove you're worthy.
You don't have to heal faster to be lovable.
You don't have to abandon yourself to be chosen.

You show up.
They show up.

Consistently.
Gently.
Honestly.

That's it.

No games.
No push-pull.
No confusion.
No withdrawal as punishment.
No breadcrumbing.

Just presence.

Real love says:

"I'm here. And I'm not going to make you earn what you already deserve."

And the first time you feel that?
It might break you open.

Not from pain.
From *relief.*
From the realization that love was never supposed to hurt like that.
From the aching awareness of everything you survived just to arrive at something soft.
From the overwhelming gratitude of finally being safe in a love that doesn't cost your soul.

It's Okay if You Don't Trust It at First

After what you've been through.
Even healthy love can feel threatening.

You'll wait for the other shoe to drop.
You'll look for signs they're like the last one.
You'll want to run — just in case.

And that's okay.

Let it be slow.
Let your nervous system adjust.
Let your guard come down on your terms.

Because the right person won't rush you.
They won't get scared of your caution.
They won't take your past personally.

They'll understand that the fact you're still showing up — even scared,
even shaky, even guarded — isn't weakness.

It's *courage.*

They won't punish your fear.
They'll respect your healing.
And they'll stay — until it feels safe to believe it's real.

They won't use your trauma against you.

They'll honor it as part of your story — not something that makes you broken, but something that makes you strong.

They'll walk with you at *your* pace, not theirs.

They'll ask what safety feels like for you — and then co-create it with you.

Real Love Isn't Perfect — But It's Repairable

It's not that you'll never fight.
It's that the fight won't be a weapon.

There's honesty.
There's repair.
There's accountability.

You're allowed to mess up.
So are they.

But the difference is:
• You're not gaslit for feeling hurt.
• You're not punished with silence.
• You're not left wondering if it's your fault.
• You don't spiral for days after a disagreement.

Because **real love wants to understand — not to win.**

Real love chooses connection over control.
Resolution over retaliation.
Truth over ego.

They don't walk away when things get uncomfortable.
They lean in.

And when they hurt you?
They care enough to change.

Not just say sorry — but actually do better.
They make it safe to stay.
And they show up even when it's messy — *especially then.*

Because that's when love is tested, and real love passes the test.
Because growth and repair are a part of love — *not* a threat to it.

Final Words for the Version of You Who Still Associates Love With Pain

You were taught love hurts.
That love means sacrifice.
That love makes you smaller.
That love is earned.
That love is conditional.

But I need you to hear this:
That was **not love**.

That was **manipulation.**
That was **survival.**
That was **trauma bonding.**
That was **abuse.**

And you don't have to keep repeating it.
You don't have to confuse struggle with devotion.
You don't have to mistake inconsistency for passion.
You don't have to settle for pain just because it's familiar.

There is love that feels like *peace.*
There is love that feels like *exhale.*
There is love that meets your softness with safety — *not exploitation.*
There is love that makes your nervous system sigh in relief — *not panic in silence.*

And most importantly:

You deserve that love.

You deserve the kind of love you used to give to the wrong people.
You deserve softness.
You deserve joy.
You deserve safe arms, warm words, and someone who doesn't make you choose between being loved... and being yourself.

And it starts with giving that love to yourself.

Completely.
Radically.
Unapologetically.

You are not hard to love.
You were just never truly loved by someone capable of holding your depth.

But now — you are becoming the kind of love you always needed.

And that changes everything.

You don't just deserve real love — *you are ready for it.*

And that truth? That's the beginning of everything.

Pause.

Take a moment to be still.
Just breathe.

I DESERVE LOVE THAT LIFTS ME UP.
I AM WORTHY OF SAFETY AND RESPECT.

Chapter Fourteen

Soft Doesn't Mean Weak — Reclaiming Vulnerability Without Losing Power

They Trained You to Fear Your Feelings

Every time you *cried*, they rolled their eyes.
Every time you *opened up*, they used it against you.
Every time you needed something, they called you *needy*.
Every time you showed emotion, they said you were *"too much."*

So you armored the f*ck up.
You *stopped crying.*
You *stopped asking.*
You *stopped letting anyone in.*

Because **softness** became dangerous.
Emotion became **ammo.**
And survival demanded **strength.**

So you became *strong.*
But not the kind that felt safe.
The kind that left you **numb.** Hardened. *Alone.*

But now?
You're *safe.*
And you don't have to live like that anymore.

You don't have to pretend you don't feel sh*t *just to protect yourself.*
*You don't have to act like your **softness** is a f*cking liability.*
Because it never was.

It was your **power** all along.
The world just told you otherwise.

The world didn't teach you how to hold that kind of power with pride. It taught you to shut it down. To bury it. To label it *weakness.*

But **softness** isn't weakness.
Softness is what kept you *human* in inhumane circumstances.
It's what tethered you to your truth when everything around you was trying to make you numb.

Softness reminded you that even when they tried to kill your spirit, they never fully succeeded.
Because something in you stayed *tender.*
And that tender part? That's your **proof.**
Proof that you made it out with your humanity intact.
And that matters.

Your **softness** was never the danger.
The danger was the world that convinced you it wasn't safe.

You survived by hardening.
But now, you **thrive** by softening.
And that shift?
That's not weakness.
That's a f*cking **revolution.**

Your Softness Is Not the Problem — Their Cruelty Was

They twisted the story.
They made you feel like you were the issue.
Too sensitive.
Too emotional.
Too deep.
Too intense.

But none of that was the problem.
The problem was them.

Your emotions made them uncomfortable because they couldn't control them.
Your vulnerability exposed their lack of depth.
Your honesty highlighted their f*cking manipulation.
Your empathy revealed their emptiness.

You weren't too much.
They were too limited.
They couldn't handle your heart —
so they tried to shut it down.

Because if they could shame your **softness**,
they'd never have to confront their own lack of it.

But here's the truth they'll never admit:

Your softness?

It scared the sh*t out of them.

Because they couldn't access that kind of depth in themselves.

And they damn sure couldn't manipulate someone who actually felt.

They feared your truth.

Because it mirrored what they refused to face in themselves.

And that's what abusers hate the most — mirrors.

They'll try to shatter you just so they don't have to see their own reflection staring back.

But that mirror isn't broken.

It's **clear**.

And it shows them everything they tried to suppress.

And you?

You kept reflecting truth even when they tried to erase you.

That takes power.

That takes heart.

That takes everything they pretend to have but don't.

They needed you to believe your heart was the problem — because they couldn't face the truth that it was their lack of one.

And now that you see that clearly?

You never unsee it again.

There Is Power in Feeling

We live in a world that rewards numbness.
Where "strong" means you keep your mouth shut.
Where "resilient" means you stuff it down until you break.
Where crying makes people uncomfortable and silence gets labeled as maturity.

But you know what the real flex is?
• Feeling your sh*t and not running from it.
• Holding space for grief without apologizing for it.
• Wanting connection and not acting like that makes you weak.
• Owning your softness and protecting it like **gold**.

You know what's brave as hell?
Still being soft when you had every reason to go cold.
Still crying when the world taught you to shut the f*ck up.
Still loving when it would've been easier to close off.
Still feeling — after everything you've been through.

Don't ever let anyone tell you that's weak.
That's **goddamn resilience.**
That's emotional courage.
That's the kind of **power** that doesn't break — it bends and comes back stronger.

That's what survivors do.

We bend.

We adapt.

But we don't lose our humanity — not even when they try to rip it out of us.

That is power.

Not just surviving the fire, but keeping your heart open afterward.

It's not about being unshakable — it's about being real.

Letting the waves hit and still choosing to stand.

Letting yourself feel everything and knowing you'll rise again anyway.

And rising with feeling?

That's not weakness.

That's proof that your spirit is still yours.

That's healing that dares to stay **soft.**

You Can Be Both Soft and Savage

You can *cry* and still cut someone off.
You can *care deeply* and still walk away without flinching.
You can be *nurturing* and still have boundaries of f*cking steel.
You can be *healing* and still that bitch.

There is nothing weak about:
• Saying *"this hurt me."*
• Needing time to process.
• Feeling *scared* to trust again.
• Walking away with tears in your eyes but your head held high.

That's **not weakness.**
That's integration.
That's what it looks like to be whole.

You are not less powerful because you feel.
You are not less worthy because you break down.

The strongest people aren't the ones who stay frozen.
They're the ones who break open and come back softer, wiser, more **dangerous —**
because now they love with intention, not desperation.

They don't *tolerate chaos.*
They *choose alignment.*

They don't *confuse softness with submission*.
They don't *perform strength*.
They **embody** it.

They know they can love you fiercely and still leave the second their boundaries are crossed.
That's a different kind of *strength*.
One that doesn't scream — but doesn't stay silent, either.

Being both soft and savage isn't contradictory — **it's divine**.
And you?
You're already living proof.

Vulnerability Isn't Giving People Power Over You — It's Reclaiming Power For Yourself

You were taught that being vulnerable meant you were exposed.
That it was **dangerous.**
That it made you a *target.*

But real vulnerability?
It's not oversharing.
It's not trauma dumping.
It's not bleeding out for people who didn't earn the right to **see you.**

It's this:

"This is how I feel.
This is who I am.
And I trust myself enough to be real — whether you get it or not."

It's not about making other people comfortable.
It's not about being understood.
It's about refusing to *hide.*

You're not giving your power away.
You're taking it the f*ck back.

Because there's nothing more terrifying to manipulative people than someone who owns their whole damn **truth.**

Someone who refuses to mask or perform.

Someone who knows that their *softness* is sacred, not shameful.

Someone who says "I trust myself more than I trust your opinion of me."

Because when your *self-trust* gets louder than their manipulation, their power crumbles.

And when you trust your truth enough to speak it out loud — even shaking, even scared — your voice becomes a weapon they can't **silence.**

And that voice? It's your **revolution.**

And it doesn't need approval. It just needs to be *yours.*

Being Soft Doesn't Mean You Let Sh*t Slide

Let's be **clear.**

Soft doesn't mean:
• You tolerate **disrespect.**
• You avoid *conflict.*
• You stay silent to keep the *peace.*
• You let someone cross your f*cking boundaries just because you "understand their trauma."

You can be *soft* and still walk away mid-sentence.
You can be soft and still say **"absolutely not."**
You can be soft and still never go back.

Softness is not *passivity.*
It's not weakness.
It's not lack of backbone.

It's **presence.**
It's compassion with a f*cking **spine.**
It's empathy without self-abandonment.
It's choosing *love* without tolerating harm.

Soft doesn't mean **weak.**
It means you're strong enough to *feel* — and still stand your ground.
It means your heart stayed open — but your standards got **sharper.**

It means you can still be moved to *tears* — and still walk the hell away from anyone who confuses that with permission.

And the ones who think *softness* means submission? Let them learn the hard way.

Because you're not here to be understood. You're here to be **respected.**

You Feel Everything — And Still Stand F*cking Tall

You cry when something hurts — and you don't apologize.
You celebrate little joys — and you don't tone it down.
You ask for support — and you don't shame yourself for *needing it.*
You say "*I love you*" — and you f*cking mean it.

You *laugh* with your whole body.
You hug like you mean it.
You let people in *slowly* — but when you do, it's real.

You don't play games.
You lead with *truth.*
You bring tenderness back into your life not out of obligation —
but because you **earned** it.

You made it through *hell* and didn't lose your ability to **feel.**
You didn't become bitter.
You didn't shut it all down.
You held on to your **humanity.**

And that tenderness? That's not your flaw — it's your f*cking **fire.**

Joy is no longer a luxury. It's your **birthright.**
You don't dilute your light to make others comfortable.
You don't apologize for being *sensitive.*

You don't shrink your laughter, your heart, or your **dreams.**
You honor them.

Because being *tender* in a world that tried to harden you —
isn't naive.
It's **powerful.**

It means you still believe in love.
It means you still believe in good.
It means you still believe in *you.*

And that kind of belief?
That's the loudest **f*ck you** to every person who tried to make you small.

Final Words for the One Who Grew Hard to Survive

You had to harden to survive.
You had to shut it down just to make it through.
You had to act like nothing hurt you when everything did.

And you made it.
That version of you?

She **saved your life.**

But now?

You're allowed to want more than *survival.*
You're allowed to want *connection* — not just protection.

You get to soften.
You get to *feel.*
You get to love like hell and still walk the f*ck away if you're not treated right.
You get to bring your whole heart into the room.
And leave if that room isn't safe.

Your *softness* is not your shame.
It's your f*cking **superpower.**

And anyone who mistakes that for *weakness*?

Is not safe for your energy.

So be *soft*.
Be *messy*.
Be *honest*.
Be *tender*.
Be f*cking unstoppable.

Because *softness* doesn't make you fragile.
It makes you **real.**

And *real* will always be more powerful than **pretend.**

And if they can't handle real? Let them keep chasing illusions.

You're done shrinking for the sake of someone else's comfort.
You're done playing small so others don't feel **insecure.**

You're not hiding anymore.
You're here. Fully. *Soft* and **sovereign.** And f*cking proud of it.

Pause.

Take a moment to be still.
Just breathe.

My softness is strength.

I am fierce, tender, and unapologetically me.

Chapter Fifteen

Boundaries Built From Fire — How to Never Abandon Yourself Again

The Truth: You Didn't Lack Boundaries — You Were Just Conditioned to Violate Them

You always had boundaries.
You just didn't know you were allowed to keep them.

Because from the start, you were taught:
- *"Be nice."*
- *"Don't make a scene."*
- *"Just let it go."*
- *"Keep the peace."*
- *"They're family."*
- *"They didn't mean it."*
- *"Stop being so sensitive."*

So you overrode your gut.
You said *"yes"* when you meant *"no."*
You made excuses for abuse.
You tolerated discomfort so they could stay comfortable.

And slowly, you learned the lie:

Keeping others happy matters more than keeping yourself safe.

You learned to people-please as protection.
To stay silent as a strategy.
To abandon your own needs before anyone else could reject them.

To morph into whatever version of yourself felt safest in the moment.

You became the peacekeeper.
The shape-shifter.
The girl who held it all in while trying to hold everyone else together.

You didn't lack boundaries.
You were never taught they were yours to honor.

And when you finally cracked under the weight of everyone else's comfort—
you were told you were the problem.

But you weren't the problem.
You were in *survival mode.*
You were exhausted.
You were human.

And now?
You're done surviving by betraying yourself.
You're done calling *self-erasure* love.
You're done being digestible to stay safe.

You're reclaiming the right to be whole—even if it makes people uncomfortable.

That Lie Ends Here

This chapter is your line in the f*cking sand.

You're done ignoring yourself to be understood.
You're done shrinking yourself to keep the peace.
You're done explaining, justifying, proving, begging, pleasing.

You're not here to be digestible.
You're here to be **whole.**

And boundaries?
They're not mean.
They're not rude.
They're not dramatic.
They're not *"too much."*
They're not something you should feel guilty about.

They are sacred self-respect in action.
They are a declaration of value—spoken without apology.
They are the quiet power move that says:

"I've betrayed myself for the last time."

Because now, you've seen what abandoning yourself leads to:
Exhaustion.
Resentment.

Emptiness.
And a haunting grief that no one else even notices.

No more.

Boundaries aren't about keeping others out.
They're about keeping you *intact.*
They're not punishment.
They're protection.

They don't push people away.
They reveal who's safe to let close.

They are the clearest declaration that *you matter too.*

You're not abandoning yourself anymore to avoid abandonment.
You're choosing you—on purpose, every time.

You're allowed to hold that line.
Even when your voice shakes.
Even when it disappoints someone.
Even when it feels unfamiliar.

Especially then.

Because every time you hold a boundary, you reinforce this truth:

You matter.

You're worth protecting.

You belong to yourself.

And no one else gets to vote on that anymore.

Boundaries Are a Language of Self-Worth

They say:
- *"I trust my feelings."*
- *"I believe in my right to peace."*
- *"I will not betray myself for your comfort."*
- *"Your reaction is not my responsibility."*
- *"My job is not to fix you."*
- *"If I lose people by being honest, they were never safe to begin with."*

That's what boundaries sound like.

Not rules.
Not threats.
Truth.

Spoken with clarity, not fear.
Held with conviction, not apology.

It's not about controlling others.
It's about protecting your f*cking peace.*

It's about saying:

"I've betrayed myself enough times. I'm not doing that again."

With each new boundary you honor—

you show yourself that you're worth keeping.

That's how you rebuild trust with yourself.
And the more you do it, the louder your self-respect becomes.

Your boundaries aren't just decisions.
They're **declarations.**

Declarations of healing.
Declarations of worth.
Declarations of a woman who is no longer available for chaos disguised as love.

You're not asking for permission anymore.
You're not seeking validation.
You're not handing your power to people who misuse it.

This is your voice.
This is your line.
This is your sacred ground.

And anyone who truly loves you—
will honor it.

You Don't Owe Access to Anyone Just Because They're Used to It

Read that again.

Just because someone's always had access to your energy, your time, your body, your heart—
does *not* mean they're entitled to it now.

Habit is not a reason to stay.
Shared blood is not a free pass.
History doesn't cancel out harm.

You're allowed to outgrow connections that require you to abandon yourself to maintain them.

You're allowed to say:
• *"I know we've always been close—but I can't keep doing this."*
• *"I know I used to say yes—but I'm not that version of me anymore."*
• *"I know they're family—but being related doesn't make them safe."*

Distance doesn't always mean hate.
Sometimes it means healing.
Sometimes love means letting go.
Sometimes peace means walking away.

And anyone who needs you to stay small in order to stay connected—

was never really connected to you in the first place.

You don't owe anyone continued access to a version of you that no longer exists.
And you don't need to apologize for choosing peace over performance.

And if the people you once gave everything to start calling you selfish?
Let them.

That's just their entitlement talking.
That's their discomfort with your healing.

You're not the villain in your story for choosing distance.
You're the **hero** for choosing peace.

You're not keeping people out.
You're just refusing to keep abandoning yourself.

Because the truth is—
you've bent over backwards to keep people close who would never do the same for you.
You've stayed quiet just to avoid their tantrums.
You've tolerated harm in the name of history.
You've given chance after chance to people who only ever took.
You've sacrificed your sanity just to avoid being called difficult.

And now you're allowed to say:

"That's enough."

That doesn't make you cold.
That makes you healed.

It means your peace finally matters more than their approval.
It means your healing is louder than their expectations.
It means you're finally showing up for the version of you that no one else protected.

That's not selfish.
That's sacred.

Guilt Is a Sign You're Breaking an Old Pattern — Not Doing Something Wrong

When you first start setting boundaries, guilt will scream.
Because your trauma taught you to associate boundaries with danger.
With punishment.
With rejection.

You'll feel selfish.
You'll feel dramatic.
You'll question yourself.
You'll want to go back to making everyone else comfortable.

But guilt isn't a sign to stop.
It's a sign you're shifting.
You're healing.
You're honoring yourself.

Let it burn.
The fire is how the old programming dies.

You're not being cruel.
You're being *clear.*
And clarity is a kindness—to you, and to everyone else.

So when guilt shows up like an old friend trying to pull you back?
Don't answer the door.

You're busy evolving.

Let guilt be proof that something sacred is changing:
You're choosing you.

And that's the most radical, rebellious act of healing there is.

That guilt is the ghost of a past version of you—the one who used to fold.
The one who kept the peace by silencing her pain.
The one who thought she had to earn rest, love, or worth.

But you're not her anymore.

Now you speak.
Now you walk away.
Now you say *"no"* and mean it.

And if your nervous system trembles, that's okay.
It's just old conditioning trying to survive in a world you've outgrown.

Let the guilt rise—then watch it pass.

Because what stands in its place is so much stronger:
Self-trust.
Self-respect.
Self-love.

And those are the roots your new life is growing from.

That's not wrong.
That's freedom.

You're Allowed to Walk Away Without a Full Explanation

You don't have to:
• Write a thesis.
• Prove your pain.
• Offer a PowerPoint on why someone was toxic.
• Stay connected to "keep things civil."

You can say:
• *"This no longer feels aligned."*
• *"I need space."*
• *"I'm done explaining myself."*
• *"This doesn't work for me anymore."*

Period.
No paragraph required.

You don't owe access.
You don't owe closure.
You don't owe clarity to the people who created your confusion in the first place.

Your boundary doesn't need to be understood.
It needs to be respected.

And if they can't?

That tells you everything you need to know.

You are allowed to outgrow the version of yourself that tolerated too much.
You are allowed to honor your needs without needing permission.
You don't have to defend your peace to the people who disrupted it.

Silence can be a boundary.
Distance can be a boundary.
Moving on without confrontation can be a boundary.

Closure doesn't have to be a conversation.
Sometimes closure is a decision:

To walk away without offering a map.
To release without seeking validation.
To choose freedom—even when they never gave you an ending.

Your healing is not a group project.
And you don't need a witness to make it real.

You're allowed to choose yourself quietly, completely, and without a single f*cking explanation.

You Don't Lose People When You Set Boundaries — You Lose Illusions

You don't lose love.

You lose control dressed as affection.

You lose obligation disguised as loyalty.

You lose manipulation hidden under *"concern."*

When you stop self-abandoning, the room gets quieter.

Some people disappear.

Others rage.

But the ones who stay?

Those are your people.

The ones who respect your "no."

Who celebrate your "yes."

Who don't make your healing about them.

Who don't see your peace as a threat to their control.

You're not losing people.

You're finding your f*cking self.*

And anyone who can't handle the real you—

was never worthy of the role they were playing in your life anyway.

Because the truth is, it was never about how lovable you were.

It was about how conditional their love always was.

They loved you when you were quiet.
When you said yes.
When you didn't challenge them.
When you put their needs first.

But when you finally chose you?
They vanished. Or punished. Or smeared.

Let them.

That's not your loss.
That's your **liberation.**

The more you love yourself, the more you see who never truly did.
The more you heal, the more obvious the harm becomes.
The more you rise, the more you realize who was trying to keep you small.

And every person who leaves when you start choosing yourself—
was making room for people who'll never ask you to dim your light just to
keep them comfortable.

Let the rest go.
Let the illusions burn.

What remains after the fire?

That's **real**.

That's **home**.

That's **yours**.

Final Words for the One Who Used to Keep the Peace at Her Own Expense

You spent years betraying your truth to protect people who wouldn't even flinch at your unraveling.

You silenced your voice.
Ignored your gut.
Abandoned your needs.
Softened your *"no"* into *"maybe."*
Laughed off what hurt you.
Swallowed your instincts so others wouldn't be uncomfortable.

Not anymore.

Now you speak your truth.
Now you walk away when it's not right.
Now you make decisions from your center—not your fear.

Your boundaries are not a defense mechanism.

They're your **return to self.**
They're your homecoming.

They're the way you say:
"I choose me."

And anyone who makes you choose between your peace and their presence?
Doesn't deserve either.

You're not the peacekeeper anymore.
You're the firestarter.

The one who said, *"That's enough."*
The one who learned to burn bridges that led back to your own self-abandonment.

You didn't become cold.
You became clear.

And now?
You never leave yourself behind again.

Pause.

Take a moment to be still.
Just breathe.

My boundaries protect me.

I choose me — every single time.

Chapter Sixteen

The Future They Never Saw Coming — Living Free, Loud, and Unapologetically You

They Thought You'd Stay Small

They never expected you to leave.
They never expected you to speak.
They never expected you to heal.

They thought if they broke you down enough, you'd give up.
They thought if they kept you questioning yourself, you'd never trust your truth.
They thought if they painted you as *"crazy,"* no one would believe your side.

They underestimated the quiet.

The way you disappeared into yourself wasn't weakness—
it was recalibration.

They thought they won.
But really?
You were just getting still enough to listen to your own voice again.

Because here you are.
Not just surviving.

Rising.

In your power.

In your voice.
In your softness.
In your fire.

Everything they tried to silence—you amplified.
Everything they mocked—you reclaimed.
Everything they feared—you became.

They thought you'd never recover.
But you didn't just recover.

You rose like a f*cking reckoning.

Stronger.
Clearer.
Louder.

And now?
You're not tiptoeing.
You're stomping.
You're not waiting for permission.
You're setting the damn standard.

You don't explain your light anymore.
You embody it.
You don't hide your scars.
You wear them like armor.

Because the truth is—
They were never scared of your wounds.
They were scared of your healing.

They were scared of what would happen when you realized you never needed their approval to begin with.

And now that you've reclaimed your power?
They can't look away.

Because everything they tried to silence is now echoing louder than their lies ever did.

They Didn't Realize You Were Taking Notes

Every insult.
Every manipulation.
Every time they made you feel like nothing—

You were taking notes.

Not for revenge.
Not for pity.

For clarity.
For boundaries.
For healing.

You were studying your pain so you could alchemize it.
You were collecting proof—not to throw back in their face,
but to hold as sacred reminders of who you'd never become.

And now?
You're the version of yourself they feared you'd become—

Because they can't reach her.
Can't shake her.
Can't shame her.

Because she's f*cking untouchable.

She's the one who learned.
The one who watched every mask slip.
The one who saw through the fake apologies, the blame-shifting, the charm turned cruelty.

She doesn't need closure.
She has truth.
She doesn't want revenge.
She has wisdom.

And she's not playing small to keep people comfortable anymore.

She's the proof that pain can birth power.
That survival can become sovereignty.
That being broken open was the very thing that made her whole.

Because every time they underestimated her, she got stronger.
And every time they tried to erase her, she carved herself deeper into existence.

She's not who they remember.
She's who they never saw coming.

They Tried to Erase You — But You Became Unforgettable

They wanted your story to stay buried.

They hoped your truth would stay hidden.

They wanted people to only remember the version of you they created—

The quiet one.

The broken one.

The one they could twist and mold.

The one who smiled through it.

The one who made it easy to keep hurting her.

But that version is gone.

Now you're loud.

Now you're bold.

Now you're real.

Now you speak before they get the chance to rewrite your truth again.

You name the abuse.

You say it out loud.

You write it.

You share it.

You own it.

You stopped protecting the people who harmed you.

You stopped editing your story to make others more comfortable.

You stopped asking for permission to speak.

You stopped shrinking for the sake of their image.

You let go of the illusion that your silence kept the peace.

Because peace built on silence isn't peace—

It's suppression.

And you weren't born to stay silent.

You were born to be a f*cking megaphone for every truth they tried to erase.

You didn't just survive their story.

You rewrote the ending.

And now?

You're unforgettable—

Not because of the pain you endured—

but because of the f*cking power you became.

You Stop Living for Their Comfort

You don't shrink to be palatable.
You don't censor yourself to protect their image.
You don't apologize for your fire.

You're no longer responsible for their reactions, their guilt, their discomfort.

You stop walking on eggshells.
You stop avoiding truth.
You stop cushioning your power just to keep them from calling you *"too much."*

You live out loud.
You take up space.
You speak with conviction.
You choose peace without permission.

And if your truth makes them uncomfortable?

Good.

Let it.

They were never meant to be comfortable in the presence of your growth.
Because your growth meant their illusion stopped working.

You stop dressing your truth in soft tones just to keep others calm.

You stop asking, *"Is this okay?"* before honoring what's true for you.

You stop holding your power hostage to avoid being labeled difficult.

Now?

You let the discomfort land where it belongs—on the people who built their comfort on your silence.

Because real healing isn't always quiet.

Sometimes it roars.

Sometimes it disrupts.

Sometimes it burns the whole damn performance down.

And when the smoke clears, you're still standing.

Not smaller. Not softer. Not sorry.

But steady. Whole. **Unapologetically true.**

You Build a Life That Feels Like Freedom

Not one that just looks good.

Not one that makes sense on paper.

Not one built from old versions of yourself who didn't know better.

This time?

You build it:

• With intention.

• With joy.

• With values.

• With boundaries.

• With people who see your light and don't try to dim it.

You stop saying yes out of guilt.

You stop explaining your no.

You stop chasing people who only showed up when you were small.

No more chaos disguised as connection.

No more obligation dressed as loyalty.

No more pressure to perform, prove, or pretend.

Just truth.

Just you.

Fully. Finally.

You make decisions that feel good in your body.
You protect your peace like it's oxygen—

Because it is.

And you realize that freedom isn't just a lifestyle.

It's a nervous system that doesn't feel like it's bracing all the time.
It's your mornings starting in stillness, not panic.
It's the space to choose instead of react.
It's saying, *"This is what I want,"* and not needing a damn permission slip.
It's feeling safe in your own skin—even when no one else gets it.
It's knowing your life isn't built to impress—

It's built to sustain.

And the people who truly love you?
They won't question your peace.
They'll protect it with you.

You Love From Wholeness — Not Wounds

You no longer seek validation from the same kind of people who once shattered you.
You've stopped falling for potential.
You've stopped craving approval.
You've stopped chasing what always ran.

You used to love from fear.
From trauma.
From desperation.
From pain.

But now?
You love from presence.
From peace.
From **wholeness.**

Now?
You attract people who meet you where you are.
Who see your scars and don't flinch.
Who hold space without trying to fix or dim you.
Who love you without conditions.

Because you finally believe you're worthy of love that doesn't require your silence.
Or your performance.

Or your self-abandonment.

You don't need to be chosen anymore.
You've already chosen yourself.

And everything good flows from that.

You stopped equating chaos with connection.
You stopped mistaking intensity for intimacy.

Now, love feels safe.
It feels calm.
It feels like being seen, not tested.

You don't need to prove your worth anymore—
You embody it.

You don't need to beg to be chosen—
You already chose yourself.

And now?
You're only available for love that honors the version of you who finally
came home.

You Become the Version of You That Scares Abusers the Most

You're no longer easily manipulated.
No longer questioning your worth.
No longer afraid to walk away.

You're self-trusting.
Self-led.
Self-loving.

And **f*cking clear.**

They don't know how to reach you anymore.
Because you don't live in fear.
You don't operate from shame.
You don't belong to their narrative.

You no longer keep the peace at your own expense.
You no longer bend just to be tolerated.
You no longer minimize your truth to avoid being labeled *"difficult."*

You are no longer silent.

And that is their worst nightmare.

Because your voice doesn't belong to them anymore.

Your choices don't revolve around their comfort.
Your energy isn't something they can drain or distort.

You're free.
And they never saw that coming.

Because they never truly saw you at all.

They don't know how to spin it now.
They can't paint you as unhinged when you're grounded.
They can't call you crazy when your clarity cuts like truth.
They can't use your empathy as a weapon, because you finally turned it inward.
They can't guilt you into silence, because you've made peace with being misunderstood.

You stopped playing the game.
And without your participation, their manipulation has nowhere to land.

You are no longer who they conditioned you to be.
You are who you chose to become.

Final Words for the Version of You They Never Expected

You used to cry on bathroom floors and wonder if you'd ever be okay again.
You used to second-guess everything.
You used to try so damn hard to be enough for people who never even saw you.

You begged for breadcrumbs.
You smiled through breakdowns.
You convinced yourself that if you could just be a little less, you'd finally be loved.

But now?

You're enough—on your own terms.
You're enough because you say so.
You're enough without their approval, validation, or f*cking presence.

You're not broken.
You're rebuilt.

You're not desperate.
You're divine.

You're not afraid.

You're f*cking alive.

And the life you're creating now?
It's the future they never saw coming—
Because they never truly saw you.

But now?
You're impossible to ignore.

You're here.
You're home.
You're whole.
And this?
This is just the beginning.

The one who used to shrink herself now expands beyond limits.
The one who was silenced now speaks with fire and grace.
The one who questioned her worth now walks like she knows she's sacred.

You are everything they tried to destroy—**and more.**
You're the storm that cleared the lies.
The light that made the shadows scream.
The voice that rose from rubble and dared to say:

"I matter."

And you do.

You always did.

Pause.

Take a moment to be still.
Just breathe.

I AM LOUD, CLEAR, AND UNAPOLOGETIC.

MY POWER CAN'T BE IGNORED.

Chapter Seventeen

You Don't Need Closure — You Need Self-Validation

Stop Chasing Closure From the Person Who Caused the Damage

Let's just say it out loud.

You're not going to get the apology you deserve.

Not the real one.
Not the one that owns every lie, every manipulation, every moment they twisted your mind and watched you break.

You won't get the tearful truth.
You won't get the, *"I finally see what I did to you."*
You won't get the moment where they come back with honesty, accountability, and awareness.

If they do come back with something?
It'll be a performance.
A half-assed explanation.
A *"sorry you feel that way."*
A tidy little version that protects their image, not your heart.

Because the kind of person who wrecked you while calling it love?
Isn't the kind of person who suddenly wakes up and decides to take accountability.

They don't want to face the truth.

They want to control the narrative.

And deep down, you already know that.
You know it in your gut.

The same place that warned you every time you silenced yourself to keep the peace.
You know it in the way your chest tightened every time they turned your tears into ammunition.
You know it in the hollow silence that came after you finally stopped begging to be understood.

You've been rehearsing closure in your head like it'll somehow rewrite history.
Like if you say the right thing or ask the right question, they'll finally say what your heart has been aching to hear.

But it's not coming.

And the longer you wait for that apology, the longer you keep yourself tied to a version of you who still thinks it's their responsibility to make it right.

The truth is, the most powerful thing you can do now is stop expecting emotional maturity from someone who built their power on your confusion.
Stop waiting for redemption from the same hands that broke you.
Stop holding your healing hostage to a moment that may never come.

Closure isn't something they'll give you.

It's something you claim when you decide your truth matters more than their lies.

Because real closure isn't a conversation.
It's a reclamation.

It's the breath you take when you realize their silence no longer defines your worth.
It's the moment your peace speaks louder than the noise they left behind.

It's not them turning around with an apology—
It's you turning inward and finally saying:

"I believe me."

You don't need their words.
You need your own.

And maybe that was the closure you were searching for all along.

Closure Is a Setup When You Expect It From Someone Who Benefited From Your Confusion

They left it messy on purpose.
The lies.
The blurred lines.
The unfinished arguments.

The way they twisted every conversation until you questioned yourself instead of them.

It wasn't just chaos—
It was control.

They knew exactly what they were doing when they made everything feel confusing.
They needed you disoriented.
Unsure.
Dependent on them for clarity.

Because if you stayed confused, you'd stay quiet.
You'd keep spinning.
Keep trying.
Keep holding on.

Because confusion was their cover.
Because the longer you stayed in a fog, the less likely you were to walk

away.

And now that you're out?
You still want that moment.

The one where they finally say,

"You were right. I treated you like shit. You didn't deserve that."

You want the weight lifted.
You want the validation.
You want to know that everything you felt wasn't just in your head.

But let's be real—

If they were capable of that kind of truth?
You wouldn't need closure.
Because you never would've been that hurt in the first place.

And maybe that's the most bitter truth of all:

The person you're waiting on to give you peace...
was the one who was always invested in your suffering.

The Real Closure Is Believing Yourself

You don't need them to explain it.
You already lived it.

You don't need to be told it was real.
You survived it in your bones.

You don't need their validation.
You need your own voice to be louder than the one they planted in your head.

Because your body remembers.
Your nervous system remembers.
Your journal remembers.

The way your voice shook when you tried to speak up—remembers.
The way you flinched when your phone lit up with their name—remembers.

The panic in your chest when they entered the room—remembers.
The emptiness after every fight that ended in your silence—remembers.

The way you questioned your reality every time they twisted your words—remembers.
The nights you laid awake trying to make sense of the chaos—remembers.

That's enough.

Closure isn't about getting their side of the story.
It's about trusting yours.

You Don't Need Their Validation to Let Go

You can let go without the justice.
You can let go without the perfect goodbye.
You can let go without the clean ending that finally makes it all make sense.

Because sometimes?
The real power move is walking away with nothing but your truth in your hands and your head held high.

You don't need to convince them of what they did.
You don't need to fix the narrative.
You don't need to wait around hoping one day they'll see it clearly.

Letting go is not giving up.
Letting go is saying:

"I'm done handing my healing to the same person who f*cked me up in the first place."

Letting go is reclaiming your power.
Not waiting for permission to move on.

It's letting the door close without needing to hear a click.
It's choosing to walk forward even when there's no apology echoing behind you.

It's giving yourself permission to stop chasing validation from a story that never honored your truth.

Because real freedom isn't found in closure.
It's found in self-trust.

It's found in the moment you decide that the version of you who kept waiting—deserves to rest.
Deserves peace.
Deserves to be free.

They Wouldn't Even Recognize the Damage If You Showed Them the Wreckage

You could spell it out.
You could hand them a breakdown of every moment they made you question reality.
You could show them your therapy notes.
The bills.
The trauma responses.
The days you couldn't eat.
The nights you shook yourself to sleep.

You could scream it.
Cry it.
Wrap it in data and details and written confessions—

And they'd still find a way to twist it.

Because people like that?
Don't deal in truth.
They deal in denial.

Your pain isn't something they'll take responsibility for—
It's something they'll use against you.

They'll call it an overreaction.
An exaggeration.

They'll say you're *"too emotional"* or *"still bitter"* or *"not over it."*

Of course you're not over it.

You're not over the lies.
You're not over the gaslighting.
You're not over how you gave your whole damn heart to someone who weaponized your love against you.
You're not over how they turned your softness into ammunition.
How they wore your empathy like a mask until it no longer served them.
You're not over how you lost pieces of yourself while trying to keep the connection alive.
How you shrank yourself to be digestible.
How your world revolved around not setting them off.

But the difference now?
You don't need them to understand it.

You're not breaking it down for them anymore.
You're done begging people to see what they're determined to ignore.

You Close the Chapter by Deciding You're Done Reopening It

This is the part that hurts the most:

The fact that they walk away fine.
That they go on like nothing happened.
That they don't lose sleep.
That they look unbothered while you're left shaking with the fallout.

And yet—

You're the one carrying the grief.
The rage.
The unanswered questions.

It's not fair.
But healing rarely is.

Closure, real closure, comes when you stop trying to make it fair.
When you stop asking, *"Why did they do this to me?"*
And start asking, *"Why am I still letting them live in my head rent-free?"*

You close the chapter not because it's complete.
But because you decide it's enough.

Because you've bled enough.

Cried enough.
Begged enough.
Explained enough.

Because every time you revisit that pain, you re-open wounds they never tried to heal.
Because your nervous system deserves more than being dragged through the same story on repeat.
Because there's power in saying:

I don't need another answer. I need peace.

This is your ending:
Not the one they gave you—
The one you give yourself.

Waking up.
Choosing you.
Walking forward.
And refusing to look back.

That's the kind of ending they'll never understand.
And the only one you'll ever need.

Final Words for the One Who Keeps Replaying the Ending

You didn't mess it up.
You didn't imagine it.
You didn't ask for it.
You didn't deserve it.

You tried.
You gave every last ounce of love you had to someone who never intended to hold it.

You over-explained.
Over-apologized.
Over-functioned.

You bent until you broke.
You stayed until it nearly killed you.
You forgave more than you should've.
You hoped longer than was fair to your own heart.

And still—

They made you feel like you were the problem.
They twisted the story so well, even you questioned your own memory.

The kind of confusion that made you stare at the ceiling night after night, wondering if you really were the problem, questioning every instinct until your confidence cracked beneath the weight of their version of events.

They acted like your pain was a performance.
They turned your boundaries into betrayal and your truth into drama.

You silenced yourself just to keep the peace.
You twisted yourself into versions that felt unrecognizable just to be tolerated.
You watered yourself down just to be digestible.
You bit your tongue until it bled.
You wore guilt like a second skin.

But that's done now.

You're done chasing peace from the same hands that shattered you.
You're done negotiating with narcissists.
You're done hoping for closure from someone who would rather keep you confused than admit they ever hurt you.

Because now you see it.

You see through the pattern.
The gaslighting.
The guilt trips.
The fake apologies.

The way they turned love into leverage.

The way they kept you close only when it benefited them.

The way they made you feel like walking on eggshells was your default setting.

The way they weaponized your empathy to keep you stuck in cycles you didn't consent to.

You stop handing them the pen to your story.

You stop letting them shape the narrative while you carry the scars.

You stop replaying the version that centers their comfort over your truth.

You stop shrinking your pain to protect their image—

and start honoring it as proof of your survival.

You stop asking people who harmed you to help you heal.

You stop explaining yourself to people committed to misunderstanding you.

You stop living your life through the lens of their denial.

You close this chapter with fire.

With fury.

With truth that doesn't tremble.

With softness that's no longer afraid to stand in its power.

Because you don't need closure.

You need you.

You need your truth—*the unedited version.*

You need your clarity—*the kind that doesn't require their confirmation.*
You need your stillness—*the kind that doesn't fear silence anymore.*
You need your peace—*the kind that comes from not needing them to under-stand a damn thing.*

That's the real ending.
Not the illusion they left you with.
Not the fake story they tried to sell the world.

But the one you write in your own voice,
with your own hands,
on your own terms.

And the beginning of everything they never wanted you to find.

You.

Whole.
Healing.
Louder than shame.
Braver than fear.
Rooted.
Rising.
Free.
Unapologetic.
Untouchable.
And fully in your f*cking power.

Pause.

Take a moment to be still.
Just breathe.

I BELIEVE MYSELF.

I RECLAIM MY PEACE WITHOUT NEEDING THEIR APPROVAL.

Chapter Eighteen

What Healing Actually Looks Like

Healing Isn't Linear — It's a F*cking Spiral

Some days, you feel free.
Other days, the memory hits like a truck.

Sometimes you're glowing.
Other times, you're dissociating in the grocery store wondering how you even got to aisle six.

One week you're journaling, drinking water, pulling oracle cards, and doing shadow work like a whole wellness influencer.
The next week you're rage-crying in the shower, eating cereal for dinner, and blocking people like it's a part-time job.

That doesn't mean you're broken.
That doesn't mean you're going backwards.

It means you're healing.

Healing isn't a checklist.
It's not a 10-step plan with a finish line.

You're not failing because you're still hurting.
You're just healing.

It's a f*cking spiral.

You come back to the same pain—
but you're not showing up the same way.

This time, you've got more tools.
More truth.
More grit.
More self-awareness.
You're not repeating cycles.
You're shedding them.

You're peeling back layers of beliefs that never belonged to you.
You're unlearning stories you were forced to live in.
You're finally facing the pain you used to numb—
sometimes shaking,
sometimes sobbing,
sometimes with your head held high.

And even when it feels like you're standing still,
when your progress feels invisible to everyone else—
It's there.
It's happening.
Because real healing doesn't always look like healing.
Sometimes it looks like mess.

But mess doesn't mean failure.
Mess means movement.

Healing Isn't Always Pretty — Sometimes It's Feral

Let's be honest—healing is raw.
It's wild.
It's so much uglier than the pastel Instagram posts make it seem.

It looks like:
• Screaming into a pillow because you've been holding it in for months
• Laughing at memes five minutes after sobbing on the bathroom floor
• Deleting their number... then checking to see if they texted anyway
• Breaking down in a parking lot because their song came on over the speakers
• Feeling guilty for smiling too soon after a breakdown
• Staring at the wall for hours because your brain won't shut up
• Repeating the same boundary 47 times because they still don't get it

It's confusing.
It's messy.
It's humbling as hell.

And most days, it's not something you'd ever post about.

But here's the thing:
There's no rulebook for this.
There's no gold star for doing it gracefully.
There's no timeline that makes it easier.

There's only your way.

And sometimes your way looks like crawling through the mud.
Sometimes it looks like canceling every plan because your nervous system is on fire.
Sometimes it looks like pretending you're okay just to get through the workday—
and falling apart when you finally close the door behind you.

It's not pretty.
It's not linear.

But it's real.

And real is enough.

You Will Miss the People Who Hurt You — That Doesn't Mean You're Not Healing

Let's say it out loud, even if it makes your stomach turn:

You're going to miss them.

You'll miss the version of them that made you feel safe.
You'll miss the good moments—
the laughs,
the routine,
the *"I love you"* texts that used to feel like home.

You'll miss the potential you clung to.
You'll miss the version of you who still had hope—
before you knew what they were capable of.

And it'll feel confusing as hell.

You'll question yourself.
You'll ask, *"What's wrong with me? Why am I still hurting over someone who hurt me?"*

But that ache?
That nostalgia?
That longing?

It doesn't mean you made the wrong choice.

It doesn't mean you're weak or naive.

It doesn't mean you're not healing.

It means you were human when you stayed.

And you're still human now that you've left.

Missing someone and choosing yourself anyway?

That's not weakness.

That's strength.

That's power.

That's growth.

You don't need to shame yourself for your grief.

You need to honor the version of you who loved through hell.

Because *she* got you here.

You Will Get Triggered — And You'll Handle It Differently Each Time

Some days, your body will panic for no reason.

You'll smell something random and be back in that awful moment.

You'll hear a tone and flinch.

You'll read a text and feel like the floor dropped out from under you.

And you'll spiral.

You'll cry.

You'll judge yourself.

You'll ask, *"Shouldn't I be over this by now?"*

But listen to me:

Triggers aren't proof that you're broken.

They're proof that your body remembers.

They're proof that you've lived through shit no one else saw.

They're evidence of your nervous system still learning what safety actually feels like.

Some days, you'll recognize it right away.

You'll ground yourself.

Breathe.

Move through it.

Other days, it'll knock the wind out of you.

And you'll shut down.

Or lash out.

Or isolate.

Both are valid.

Both are part of healing.

Both are part of the spiral.

You don't fail because you got triggered.

You're not *"starting over"* because you had a setback.

You're human.

And your healing doesn't disappear just because you had a rough day.

Healing Doesn't Mean You Forgive Everyone — It Means You Stop Needing Closure From Them

You don't have to forgive people who aren't sorry.
You don't have to spiritualize your trauma.
You don't owe softness to the people who hardened you.

Sometimes healing looks like:
• Staying angry longer than you're *"supposed to"*
• Holding a boundary without overexplaining it
• Going no contact and not feeling bad about it
• Refusing to make peace with chaos just because it's familiar

You're not here to make other people comfortable with the damage they caused.
You don't have to wrap your pain in a bow for someone else's peace.

You don't heal by minimizing your hurt.
You heal by telling the f*cking truth.

And sometimes the truth is ugly.
Sometimes it's bitter.
Sometimes it's no contact forever.

That's not bitterness.
That's protection.
That's wisdom.

You Will Outgrow People, Habits, and Versions of You That Once Felt Like Home

Healing means letting go—
of the old roles,
the old masks,
the old survival tactics you used to call strength.

Letting go of the survival self who smiled through abuse.
Letting go of the friendships that only survived your silence.
Letting go of the parts of you that were created just to be accepted.

And that?
It will hurt.

Because even survival patterns feel like home when you've lived in them long enough.
Even dysfunction feels safe when it's what you've always known.

So when you walk away from that?
It will feel like grief.

You're grieving the quiet version of you.
The one who didn't speak up.
The one who dimmed her light.
The one who tolerated less so she could feel like enough.

But here's the plot twist—

You're also becoming.

You're becoming the version of you who doesn't need to shrink.

The one who says no.

The one who walks away.

The one who knows her worth even when no one else claps for it.

That's the kind of growth no one talks about.

The kind that feels like heartbreak and rebirth at the same time.

You Learn to Celebrate the Little Things — Because You Know What It Took to Get Here

You start to notice the tiniest shifts:

• When you say *"I'm not okay"* and don't feel ashamed
• When you take a nap instead of powering through
• When you feel joy without waiting for it to disappear
• When you walk away without needing one more red flag
• When you rest—and don't call it laziness

These are the moments no one else sees.

The ones that don't make headlines.
The ones that feel too small to celebrate—

But you know.

You know how hard it was to get here.
You know what it took just to function.
You know how many times you almost gave up and didn't.

Celebrate that.
Celebrate you.
Celebrate the quiet wins.

Because they matter more than anyone realizes.

Final Words for the One Who Thinks She's Not Healing Fast Enough

You're not behind.
You're not broken.
You're not doing it wrong.

You're just doing something impossible—

Undoing years of gaslighting.
Rewiring a nervous system that's been stuck in survival.
Grieving the self you used to be while trying to build a new one.

And no one talks about how f*cking hard that is.

You're not meant to be *"fixed."*
You're meant to be free.
You're meant to feel safe in your own skin again.

And it takes time.
It takes patience.
It takes showing up for yourself over and over again—
even when you're tired of trying.

You don't need to be a storybook version of recovery.
You don't have to have it all together.

You just have to keep going.

Even when it's dark.
Even when it's lonely.
Even when it's f*cking unfair.

Because healing isn't a straight line.
It's a spiral.
A sacred one.

Every loop teaches you something your trauma once tried to erase.
You come back to the pain not because you're failing—

But because you're stronger now.
Wiser now.
More self-loving now.

You're not spiraling.
You're ascending.

Layer by layer.
Wound by wound.
Truth by truth.

And this spiral?
It's your way back home—

To your voice.
To your power.
To your peace.
To your f*cking freedom.

Pause.

Take a moment to be still.
Just breathe.

HEALING IS MESSY AND REAL.

I'M DOING THE WORK, EVEN ON HARD DAYS.

Chapter Nineteen

The Peace You Paid for in Pain

This Isn't Just Peace. This Is Aftermath.

This isn't the kind of peace people talk about when they say,
"Just let it go."
"Move on."
"Don't hold onto it."

This is the kind of peace that came after you almost didn't make it.

The kind that came after the begging, the confusion, the spirals, the shame.
The kind that showed up after you cried on your bathroom floor for the third night in a row.

After you deleted the same number fifteen times but still memorized it by heart.
After you whispered, *"I can't do this anymore,"* and meant it.
After you sat on the edge of your bed at 2 a.m., gripping your chest, wondering if the pain would ever stop.

This peace cost you everything:
• Your voice.
• Your energy.
• Your self-worth.
• Your sense of safety.
• Your f*cking identity.

So no—

You don't owe anyone an explanation for why you protect it now like your life depends on it.

Because it does.

You Didn't Just Heal — You Rebuilt

This peace came from:
• Burning bridges that needed to collapse.
• Saying no when your voice shook.
• Losing people who never truly saw you.
• Grieving the version of you who stayed too long.
• Facing the ugliest truths—and choosing to keep going anyway.

You didn't just *"get better."*
You clawed your way out of hell with nothing but your own intuition, your tears, and a barely-there belief that life could be different.

You made coffee while sobbing.
You dropped your kids off at school and smiled, even when your insides felt like glass.
You sat in your car, numb, staring at the steering wheel for 45 minutes before finally driving home.
You kept showing up to work while your heart felt like it was in pieces.
You raised your kids, brushed your hair, replied to messages—when what you really wanted was to disappear.
You did the damn dishes while silently falling apart.
You answered texts with emojis because you couldn't explain the war inside your head.
If you even answered them at all.

And now?

This peace is the reward for every time you didn't give up.

For every time you made the impossible choice to keep breathing.

To keep hoping.

To keep moving, even when it felt like no one saw you bleeding.

This Peace Isn't Passive — It's Rooted and Unshakable

This peace didn't come from *"letting it go"* or pretending it didn't hurt.
It came from feeling all of it.

It came from facing every truth you used to deny.
From revisiting every memory you swore you'd buried.
From finally admitting to yourself that it was abuse—*even when no one else would say it.*

It came from crying through the nights no one knew about.
From rereading old messages to remind yourself you weren't crazy.
From deleting screenshots, redownloading them, then staring at them again just to make sure it wasn't in your head.
From walking away from people you once would've begged to stay.

It came from pretending to be okay while your world was falling apart—
because you didn't have the luxury of falling apart.
It came from answering work calls with a steady voice while your heart felt like it was breaking in the background.
It came from nights where you couldn't even cry because you were too numb to feel anything at all.
It came from the moments you almost said something—
but swallowed the truth instead, because you knew they'd twist it anyway.

This peace is not weakness.
It's not apathy.
And it's definitely not the absence of feeling.

It's what happens when your nervous system finally stops bracing for impact.

When your heart doesn't skip a beat every time your phone buzzes.

When you stop scanning every room for exits—

because you finally feel safe in your own f*cking life.

It's when your body finally exhales.

And this time, for real.

It's clarity.

The kind that says:

- *"I don't need to explain myself to be understood."*
- *"I don't let people back into my life just because they say the right things."*
- *"I don't betray my body's wisdom for someone else's comfort."*
- *"I can care deeply—and still choose distance."*

This peace isn't performative.

It doesn't need approval.

It doesn't come with disclaimers or justifications.

It's quiet.

But it's powerful.

Because it knows what it cost you to earn it.

You didn't become cold.

You became clear.

And now:

You don't chase chaos pretending it's love.

You don't confuse familiarity with safety.

You don't make yourself small to stay connected.

You don't shrink anymore just to be tolerated.

You don't pretend you're okay just to be liked.

You don't stay silent just to avoid tension.

This peace doesn't bite.

It simply doesn't bend.

You Don't Apologize for Choosing Peace Over People

You've lost enough.
You've hurt enough.
You've done enough explaining, fixing, tolerating.

You've watched people leave just because you finally spoke your truth.
You've been called bitter, angry, too much, not enough—
just for choosing yourself.

But here's the thing:

You don't owe anyone access to your healed self if they only knew how to love your broken one.
You remember who checked in—
and who disappeared.
Who cared when it was hard—
and who only showed up when you were easy to be around.

Read that again.

You can love people from a distance.

You can care and still walk away.

You can wish them well without ever letting them near you again.

Because closure doesn't mean reconnection.

Forgiveness doesn't mean re-entry.

And peace doesn't mean people-pleasing.

That's peace.
That's power.
And that's yours now.

The Right People Will Never Make You Compromise Your Peace to Keep Them

Let's be honest:

Some people were never going to love you unless you were shrinking, suffering, or silent.
Unless you were easy to control.
Easy to manipulate.
Easy to mold into what they needed you to be.

But now?

You're not easy to f*ck with.
You're not easy to gaslight.
You're not easy to guilt into staying.
You're not easy to fool with pretty words and empty promises.

Because now you listen to your body.
You honor your limits.
You protect your peace like it's sacred—

Because it f*cking is.

You trust the red flags now.
You don't override your instincts.
You no longer betray your own soul just to keep someone else comfortable.

And the ones who get to stay in your life?

They're the ones who respect your peace.

Not the ones who demand you dim it.

Final Words for the One Who Doesn't Recognize Herself in the Mirror — And That's a Good Thing

You used to be chaos.
Now you're calm.

You used to be fear.
Now you're fire.

You used to be survival mode.
Now you're a force.

You used to beg for breadcrumbs.
Now you build your own table.

You used to tiptoe around other people's moods.
Now you walk boldly in your truth.

You used to wonder if you were too much.
Now you know you were just too real for the wrong people.

You used to ask, *"What's wrong with me?"*
Now you ask, "Why did I ever let them convince me I was the problem?"

And sure—some people will say you've changed.
Some will say you're *"cold now"* or *"too guarded"* or *"not who you used to be."*

Let them.

They never knew the real you.
They only knew the version you became to survive them.

Good.

You're not.
You shouldn't be.

You earned this version of you.

You paid for her in panic attacks and silent screams and nights where you couldn't even recognize your own reflection.
You paid for her in the breakdown you had while folding laundry.

In the grocery aisle where you suddenly couldn't breathe.
In the moment you sat in your driveway because going inside felt too heavy.

You paid for her in every breakdown, every emotional crash, every moment you thought about giving up.
You paid for her in silence.

In isolation.
In every time you held it all in because you didn't want to be a burden.

This is who you were always meant to be—
before the world taught you to dim your light just to stay loved.

So don't you dare apologize for her.
Don't let anyone make you feel guilty for becoming the version of you that finally feels safe in her own skin.

This peace?

It's your home now.

And no one gets to burn it down again.

Pause.

Take a moment to be still.
Just breathe.

MY PEACE IS HARD-EARNED AND SACRED.

I PROTECT IT FIERCELY.

Chapter Twenty

This Is What a Free Woman Sounds Like

She Doesn't Ask for Permission Anymore

She used to check herself.
Filter herself.
Edit every sentence to soften the impact.

She used to scan the room, measure reactions, overthink her tone—
her stomach knotting with every pause in the conversation,
bracing for a shift in someone's energy—
and replay every conversation in her head before bed.

She used to wonder:
"Is this too much?"
"Will they be mad?"
"What if they leave?"

She spent years molding herself into something easier to swallow—
softer, quieter, more agreeable.

And for what?

To be dismissed anyway.
To be lied to anyway.
To be left anyway.

Now?

She doesn't care who leaves—
as long as she doesn't leave herself again.

She speaks without flinching.
She says no without guilt.
She claims space like she was born to take it.

Because she was.

She doesn't minimize her needs just to be chosen.
She doesn't over-explain just to be understood.
She doesn't beg people to treat her like a human being anymore.

That version of her is gone.
Buried under every time she betrayed her own truth just to keep the peace.

This version?
She is the peace.

She speaks even when her voice shakes.
She stays seated at the table even when her hands tremble—
because staying silent hurt more.

She's not looking for approval anymore—
she's reclaiming her place.

She remembers the nights she stood frozen in the hallway,
phone in hand,
rehearsing what she wanted to say—
but saying nothing.

She remembers editing texts ten times,
deleting truths,
and settling for crumbs.

Now?

She hits send without a second thought.
She speaks,
and if they can't hold the weight of her voice,
that's not her problem anymore.

Her Voice Doesn't Shake Because She's Angry—It Shakes Because She's Powerful

They always called her *"emotional."*
"Too much."
"Too intense."

They said she was dramatic for crying when she was hurt.
Cold for pulling away when she was disrespected.
Crazy for reacting to chaos they created.

But now?

She lets her emotion fuel her clarity.
She doesn't shrink for comfort.
She doesn't water herself down.
She doesn't let fear drive the car.

She walks in the room and doesn't question if she belongs.

She already knows—because she built the damn room.

And if it wasn't made for her?
She'll burn it and start over.

They called it *"anger."*
She calls it knowing better now.

They called her *"difficult."*
She calls it: not manipulatable.

They said she was *"scary."*

She says: maybe you should be scared of a woman who finally realized her worth.

She used to bite her tongue until it bled.

Now she bites back—
with truth.
With boundaries.
With fire that doesn't ask for permission to exist.

There were days she'd sob into her steering wheel just for being talked over in a meeting.
Times she'd sit on the bathroom floor with her mouth open—
but no words coming out—
because she'd been silenced so many times, she forgot how to scream.

But now?

Now her voice doesn't need to be loud to be powerful.

It's in the calm refusal.
The unshaking *"no."*
The silence that follows someone crossing a line.

That silence used to feel like weakness—

Now it's power.

She No Longer Feels Bad for Being Hard to Manipulate

Let them say she's *"cold"* now.
Let them say she's *"guarded."*
Let them say she's *"changed."*

She has.

Because warmth was never the problem.
It was the people who kept freezing her out and expecting her to stay soft anyway.

She got tired of being twisted.
Tired of being erased.
Tired of proving she was worth decency.
Tired of performing for people who were never clapping for her.

So now?

She no longer explains.
She no longer justifies.
She no longer entertains conversations that demand she abandon herself to be understood—
with people who showed her they were never listening.

You don't get to call her bitter when she's finally just clear.

She doesn't ignore her intuition to be *"nice."*
She doesn't betray her nervous system just to avoid being misunderstood.

She doesn't owe anyone access to the version of her that sacrificed herself to be loved.

She's not a cold woman.
She's a woman with boundaries.

And the only people who confuse the two—
Are the ones who benefited from her not having any.

She used to fold herself smaller just to keep the room comfortable.
Now she walks in, fully expanded—

And if the space can't hold her, she leaves.

She no longer turns herself into a contortionist just to keep the peace.
She doesn't respond to messages that feel like bait.
She doesn't show up to prove she's *"not difficult."*
She lets people misunderstand her—

And keeps walking anyway.

That's not rudeness.
That's liberation.

That's no longer needing to play by the rules of people who only made her feel like sh*t.

She Isn't Just Healed—She's Aware

Healing isn't some magical land where nothing hurts anymore.
It's not constant peace and soft playlists and daily journaling under moon-
light.

It's a grounded awareness that says:

"I see the red flags now.
I feel the shift in my body.
And I walk away before the damage is done."

That's freedom.

Not ignoring the gut feeling.
Not bypassing discomfort for the sake of appearances.
But trusting herself so deeply that she doesn't need anyone else to confirm
what she already knows.

It's self-trust.
It's clarity.
It's peace that no one else owns anymore.

That kind of peace doesn't just happen.
It's earned.
It's rebuilt from the ground up—
through every breakdown, every spiral, every single time she caught herself
and kept going.

It's remembering what it felt like to pretend to be okay—
With mascara on her cheeks,
the scent of leftover detergent clinging to her hoodie,
and a forced smile at dinner.

And deciding she's never going back.

And that peace?
It echoes in everything she says and does.

You can hear it in her laugh.
You can feel it in the way she holds her boundaries—
calm, steady, without flinching.
You can see it in her silence.
You can sense it in the way she doesn't chase closure anymore.

Because when a woman gets free?
Her energy speaks before she even opens her mouth.

Freedom isn't about being unaffected—
It's about being unf*ckwithable.

It's sitting across from someone trying to twist your reality—
And not even blinking.
It's walking away from what you prayed would work—
Because you finally love yourself more than the fantasy.

It's having the self-respect to say, *"This isn't love,"* and mean it.

Even when it hurts.
Especially when it hurts.

Her Story Isn't a Secret—It's a Weapon She Wields With Purpose

She used to hide it.
The trauma.
The heartbreak.
The breakdowns.
The spirals.

The way she stayed in rooms that were burning—
and kept pretending it wasn't smoke in her lungs.

She thought being *"strong"* meant pretending none of it happened.

So she smiled when she wanted to scream.
She performed while falling apart.
She carried the weight quietly because she didn't want to burden anyone.

Now?

She tells the truth.
Not for pity.
Not for shock value.

But for the ones who still think they're alone in it.

The ones sitting on their bathroom floor wondering if it's just them.
The ones who wake up with swollen eyes and silence in their chest,
wondering if anyone would notice if they disappeared.
The ones who are still being gaslit and called crazy for reacting to abuse.

The ones who keep shrinking because they were never taught they were allowed to take up space.

Her story isn't a scar—
It's a signal.

She is the validation.
She is the proof.
She is the reminder:

You can survive hell and still become someone beautiful.

And even when you don't feel beautiful?
You're still worthy of being seen.

She doesn't need a stage—
She just needs truth.

Her voice cracks sometimes,
but it still reaches the ones who need it.

She's the kind of woman who tells her story before someone else can twist it.
She's the voice that says, *"Me too"* before you even speak.

She's the proof that even when you break into a thousand f*cking pieces—
Your truth can still echo louder than their lies.

She used to protect their reputations.
Now she protects her own peace.

Final Words for the One Who Thought She'd Never Be Free

This is for the woman who stayed silent for too long.
For the girl who blamed herself.
For the version of you who was afraid to take up space.
For the survivor who still flinches at the sound of their name.

You made it out.
You made it through.
You made yourself—again.

And maybe no one saw it happen.
Maybe it didn't look like a movie moment.
Maybe it was just you, sitting alone in your car, fists clenched around the steering wheel, whispering, *"Just one more day."*

But that day turned into another.
And another.

And here you are.

And now?

You speak.
You roar.
You rest.
You create.
You love—on your own terms.

You stopped performing and started living.

You stopped surviving and started choosing.

You remember the version of you who whispered, *"I can't do this anymore,"*
with mascara on her pillow and shame in her chest.

And now you rise with a voice that doesn't shake.

You don't have to explain your softness.

You don't have to defend your strength.

You don't need anyone's permission to be who the f*ck you are.

You are not too much.

You are not too broken.

You are not too anything.

You are free.

And your voice?

It's what freedom f*cking sounds like.

You are what this book was always about.

Not perfection.

Not peace that never cracks.

But truth.

Power.

Reclamation.

You were stripped down—
piece by f*cking piece.

And somehow,
you made art out of every scar.

This isn't your ending.
It's your emergence.

And no one gets to silence you ever again.

Pause.

Take a moment to be still.
Just breathe.

I SPEAK MY TRUTH WITHOUT PERMISSION.

I AM FREE, FIERCE, AND WHOLE.

This is what healing looks like—piece by f*cking piece.*

Closing Words — For the Ones Who Get It

If you made it this far, you've already done something powerful.

You've sat in the dark with someone who knows what it feels like to lose yourself.
To question your sanity.
To beg for crumbs—
and still be blamed.

To be so far gone you didn't think you'd ever come back.

But here you are.

No, this book won't fix it all.
But maybe it reminded you that you're not crazy.
Not too sensitive.
Not broken.
Not unworthy.

You were abused.
And you are still here.

That matters more than they'll ever know.

Don't rush to be okay.
Don't force yourself to forgive what you haven't even fully processed yet.
And don't let anyone tell you how long healing is supposed to take.

You don't need to be inspirational to be valid.

You just need to keep choosing yourself—
every day,
even when it's messy.

Healing is personal.

But it's also a rebellion.

You don't owe them silence anymore.

With you in the dark, and on the way out—
Lindsay-Michele

About the author

Lindsay-Michele didn't grow up around abuse.

She didn't expect to fall into it.

But she did — again and again — and it destroyed her.

She was emotionally, verbally, physically, and sexually abused in different relationships over the years.

Manipulated. Silenced. Erased.

Expected to keep showing up, smiling, functioning — all while carrying trauma alone.

This book isn't her story.

It's the truth she never got to say when it was happening.

It's the pain she carried in silence.

The reality of what abuse actually feels like — and what it really takes to survive it.

She created *Down the Rabbit Hole* because no one warned her how lonely it would be.

No one handed her a book that made her feel understood.

No one showed her what healing actually looks like — the rage, the spirals, the shut downs, the shame, the days you barely make it out of bed.

And that kind of isolation almost killed her.

So now?

She writes, she speaks, and she shares the truth — not to inspire, but to **make sure no one else feels as alone as she did.**

She's not here to pretend healing is pretty.
She's here to show you that **you're not broken,** you're not dramatic, and you're not crazy —
You're just healing from **sh*t** no one talks about.
And she's walking it with you — piece by **f*cking** piece.

You can find her work at www.lindsay-michele.com or on Instagram @downtherabbithole.lm.

Resources Page

If you're in crisis or need support, here are some resources that may help:

Crisis Support
- National Domestic Violence Hotline: 1–800–799–SAFE (7233)
- RAINN (Sexual Assault Support): 1–800–656–HOPE (4673)
- 988 Suicide & Crisis Lifeline: Call or text 988

Therapy & Mental Health
- www.psychologytoday.com – Find licensed therapists
- www.opencounseling.com – Free or low-cost counseling options

Books & Tools That May Help
- *The Body Keeps the Score* by Bessel van der Kolk
- *What My Bones Know* by Stephanie Foo
- Meditation, journaling, and somatic healing tools

Invitation to Connect

If this book made you feel seen — even in the smallest way — I'd love to hear from you.

Your story matters.
Your pain is valid.
You deserve to be supported by people who actually get it.

You can connect with me here:
• Website: www.lindsay-michele.com
• Instagram: @downtherabbithole.lm
• Email: lindsay@lindsay-michele.com

For collaborations, interviews, or stocking inquiries:
• Email: lindsay@lindsay-michele.com